Francis Grose

The Antiquities of Scotland

Vol. 2

Francis Grose

The Antiquities of Scotland
Vol. 2

ISBN/EAN: 9783337324742

Printed in Europe, USA, Canada, Australia, Japan

Cover: Foto ©ninafisch / pixelio.de

More available books at **www.hansebooks.com**

The Antiquities of Scotland

By Francis Grose Esq: F.A.S.^{s}

of London and Perth.

THE SECOND VOLUME

LONDON Printed for HOOPER & WIGSTEAD N.º 212 High Holborn.
MDCCXCVII.

GALLOWAY.

LINCLUDEN COLLEGE. Plate I.

The college of Lincluden, in Galloway, ſtands upon the water of Cluden, where it falls into the river Nith, about two miles above or north of Dumfries. This houſe was originally a priory of Benedictine nuns, founded in the reign of King Malcolm IV., by Uthred, father to Rolland, Lord of Galloway, who was buried here. By him Lincluden was endowed with the divers lands lying within the baronies of Corſe Michael and Drumfleith, in the ſtewartry of Kirkcudbright. The particulars are mentioned in the notes below.* This priory was afterwards changed by Archibald the Grim, Earl of Douglas, Lord of Galloway and Bothwell, Panitarius Scotiæ, into a college or provoſtry, confiſting of a provoſt and twelve beadſmen, becauſe of the lewd and ſcandalous lives of the nuns.† This Earl died A. D. 1400, and was interred in the ſacriſty

---

* The five merkland
- of Little Dryburgh
- of Drumjarg
- of Eruphillan
- of Erncraig
- of Blarome
- of Meikle Dryburgh
- of Chriſſmanton
- of Blacharne
- of Erne Menzie
- Culnotrie

The corn mill of Corſe Michael.
The five merkland of Garrenton.
The two and half merkland of Black Park.

All lying within the barony of Corſe Michael and ſtewartry of Kirkcudbright.

The fifteen-ſhilling land of Stackford
The forty-ſhilling land of Newton
The merkland of Clunie and Skellingholm
The ſix merkland of Carraſehtie, or Carnchan
The ſix merkland of Drumganis
The five merkland of Traquier
The merkland of Stockholm
The five merkland of Nunland
The five merkland of Cruiſtanes, or Curriſtains
The ſix merkland of Holm, now Goldee Lee
The twenty-ſhilling land of Maryholm
The four merkland of Nunholm,

All lying within the barony of Drumſleith and ſtewartry of Kirkcudbright.

† Alienore Prioureſſe de Lincluden del Conte de Dumfries is mentioned by Prynne, ad annum 1296.

or veftry here; over the door of which are ftill to be feen his and his lady's armorial bearings; fhe was heirefs of Bothwell; they are neatly carved in ftone on different fhields; between which three ftars are interlaced with three cups, the latter are the infignia of his office of Panitarius Scotiæ.

THE name of the firft provoft of this college was Elefe. He was fucceeded by Alexander Cairns, appointed by Earl Archibald the fourth, whofe chancellor he appears to have been, being, by a charter of that Earl, dated February 12, 1413, thus defcribed: Alexander de Carnys, Præpofius de Lincluden Cancellarius nofter. In the year 1422 he was fucceeded by John Cameron, official of Lothian,* and rector of Cambuflang, who was confeffor and fecretary to archibald, the fourth Earl of Douglas, above mentioned. This John Cameron, on the reftoration of James I., was named Secretary and Lord Privy Seal, and the year following was appointed keeper of the great feal; he was foon after elected bifhop of Glafgow; and, in 1429, was appointed one of the commiffioners from Scotland for redreffing grievances, and fettling the peace with England: foon after, with the confent of their refpective patrons, he made the minifters of the churches of Cambruflang, Torbolton, Eglesham, Kirkmahoe, Lufs, and Kilearn, prebendaries of Glafgow, to have ftalls within the choir there, and places and votes in the chapter for ever. Among the lift of patrons was, Sir John Forrefter, of Corfterfin, patron of Kirkmahoe, in right of his wife, Margaret: fhe, with the confent of her fon and heir, Sir William Stewart, agreed to it.

IN the year 1433, Cameron was appointed one of the delegates from Scotland to the Council of Bafil; to which place he went through England with a retinue of thirty perfons in his train.

IN 1437, when the peace was to be negociated with England, Cameron was one of the Plenipotentiaries for Scotland, and had a fafe conduct for that purpofe to pafs into England, together with Sir Alexander Seaton, Sir Walton Ogilvie, and Sir John Forrefter. After the murder of James I. Cameron was removed from the office of Chancellor, when

---

* An official was one appointed to a See, but not confirmed by the Pope.

he

he returned to his bifhoprick, and built the great tower of the Epifcopal palace at Glafgow, on which his efcutcheon of arms is placed; he alfo laid out a great fum of money in rebuilding the veftry, which his predeceffor, bifhop Lauder, had begun.

In the year 1439, in an indenture between Jean, widow of James I., and Sir Alexander Livingfton, of Callender, anent the perfon of James II. among the numerous feals appendant to that deed was that of Cameron. He died at Lockwood on Chriftmas Eve, A. D. 1446.

Cameron was fucceeded in his provoftry of Lincluden by Halyburton, whofe arms are to be feen on the fouth walls, within the choir.

He was fucceeded by John Methuin, doctor of the decretals, who, in 1437, during the minority of James II., was fecretary of Scotland, and one of the plenipotentiaries along with Sir John Forrefter, of Corfterfin, lord chamberlain of Scotland, the Lords Gordon and Montgomery, with Sir Vano, or Vans: they met at London in time of open war, and, in 143?, renewed the truce for nine years.

In 1444 Methuin was difmiffed from his office of fecretary, and died foon after. He was fucceeded by provoft Lindfay in 1449, who, in 1465, was appointed lord privy feal; and, along with Muirhead, bifhop of Glafgow; Spence, bifhop of Aberdeen; Crawford, abbot of Holyrood Houfe; the Earls of Crawford, of Argyle; the Lord Livingftone, Chamberlaine, and Alexander Boyd, of Duncow, was fent ambaffador to England to redrefs all grievances. This commiffion is dated in 1465.

Upon the 18th of December, 1468, William, Earl of Douglas, affembled all the lords, barons, and freeholders, with the oldeft borderers at Lincluden, to revife the border laws, when divers regulations were made. Lindfay was fucceeded in the provoftry of Lincluden by Livingftone, who was fucceeded by William Herries, rector of Kirkpatrick, who was one of the attendants upon James, the ninth Earl of Douglas, when upon his pilgrimage to Rome, in 1453.

Provost Anderson fucceeded Herries; and Anderfon's fucceffor was William Stewart, fecond fon to Sir Thomas Stewart, of Minto, who was fecond fon to Sir Alexander Stewart, of Garlies. This provoft Stewart was formerly rector of Lochmaban; he was afterwards bifhop of Aberdeen, and appointed lord treafurer of Scotland;

his arms are still to be seen under the Scots arms, upon the great staircase in the provost's lodgings here, which he either rebuilt, or very much repaired. He was afterwards succeeded by provost Maxwell, whose successor was Robert Douglas, second son to the baron of Drumlanrig; to him —— Douglas, of Drumlanrig, who was succeeded by John Douglas, of Boatford, who was the last provost, when Lincluden became a temporal barony in 1565; since which period it has been the property of the Nithsdale family. From what remains of that ancient building, which is part of the provost's house, the chancel, and some of the South wall of the church, an idea may be easily formed of its former splendour. The choir in particular was finished in the finest style of the florid Gothic, The roof was treble, in the manner of that of King's college at Cambridge, and the trusses, from whence the ribbed arch-work sprung, are covered with coats of arms; the lower roof is now entirely demolished; the middle one, a plane arch, still stands; but the uppermost roof, which consisted of timber and lead, was destroyed at the Reformation. The Earls of Douglas, when in the zenith of their power and greatness, expended considerable sums in ornamenting this place, which was their favourite residence, when wardens of the west marches. In the chancel is the elegant tomb of Margaret, daughter of Robert III. wife of Archibald, Earl of Douglas, first Duke of Terouan, and son of Archibald the Grim. Her effigy, at full length, says Mr. Pennant, lay on the stone, her head resting on two cushions; but the figure is now mutilated, and her bones, till lately, were scattered about in a most indecent manner, by some wretches who broke open the repository in search of treasure. The tomb is in the form of an arch, with all parts most beautifully carved: on the middle of the arch is the heart, the Douglass's arms, guarded by three chalices,* set crossways, with a star near each, and certain letters I could not read. On the wall is inscribed, *A L'aide de dieu*, and at some distance beneath, *Hic Jacet D-na* Margareta *regis* Scotiæ *filia quodam Comiiffa de* Douglas *Dna* Gollovidiæ *et vallis Annandiæ.*

---

* These are generally supposed to be cups, the insignia of his office of cupbearer of Scotland, and not chalices.

In

Linlithgow College Pl.

GALLOWAY.

In the front of the tomb are nine shields, containing as many arms: in one are the three stars, the original coat of this great house, for the heart was not added till the good Sir James was employed in carrying that of Robert Brus to the holy land; besides these are the arms after that event; and also their arms as Lords of Annandale, Galloway and Liddesdale. Near the tomb is a doorcase, richly ornamented with carving; and on the top the heart and cups, as in the former.

In other parts of the remains of this church are the arms of the Douglases, or Dukes of Terouan, Earls of Angus, of Ormond, and of Murray: here are besides, the arms of John Stewart, Earl of Athol, with the motto, *firth, fortune,* and *fil the fetters.*

Beneath one of the windows are two rows of figures, the upper of angels, the lower of a corpse and other figures, all much defaced, but seemingly designed to express the preparations for the interment of our Saviour.

The remains of a bowling-green and flower-garden, with the parterres and scrolls, very visible, still exist on the south-east side of the building: beyond which is a great artificial mount, with a spiral walk to the top, which is hollowed, and has a turf seat around, whence there is a most delightful view over the adjacent country, to which the junction of the rivers is no small addition.

This view, which shews the south-west aspect, was drawn A.D. 1789.

LINCLUDEN COLLEGE. Plate II.

This plate exhibits the ruin as it appears from nearly the north-east aspect. The building at the end next the spectator was the provost's tower, or mansion. It was drawn A. D. 1789, a few months after the former.

THRIEVE, OR THRIEFF, CASTLE.

This castle stands upon an island of sixteen Scots acres, formed in the river Dee, in Galloway. Here was, it is said, a more ancient fortress belonging to the old Lords, or petty Kings, of Galloway; which being demolished, the prefent building was erected, but by whom, or when is not afcertained, but fuppofed to be by a Douglas. Tradition fays, this caftle obtained the appellation of Th'rive's Caftle, that is, the caftle of the Rive, from one of the Lords of Galloway, of that family, who refided here; and, from his depredations and extortions, was called the Rive: others derive it from the word *Reeve*, as being a contraction of the Reeves Caftle.

Upon the ruin of the houfe of Douglas, and the annexation of the Lordfhip of Galloway to the crown of Scotland in 1455, this caftle remained in the King's hands, who appointed captains for the keeping thereof, as occafion required. In the year 1502, Sir John Dunbar, of Mochrum, was appointed keeper of the caftle of Thrieff for nine years, and the twenty-five merks worth of land, called the Granges of Thrieff, and the fifhery thereof, with all other profits and duties whatfoever, pertaining to the faid caftle, with the office of fteward, of the ftewartry of Kirkcudbright, for which he was to pay the King yearly, on Whitfunday and Martinmas, the fum of one hundred pounds, and to keep up the caftle at his own charge. This grant was dated the 12th of September. But in the year 1524, it appears by another grant dated at Edinburgh, September 9th, that this caftle, with that of Loughmaban, with all their perquifites and appendages, and all the King's lands at Duncow, within the county of Dumfries, together with the office of fheriff of Kirkcudbright, with all its profits and fees, were given to Robert, Lord Maxwell, and the longeft liver of his fons, and their affigns and tenants, for the fpace of nineteen years from the feaft of St. Martin.

The Lords Maxwell, afterwards Earl of Nithfdale, poffeffed the heritable office of ftewards, of the ftewarty of Kirkcudbright, and keepers of the caftle of Thrieff, until the year 1747, when all the heritable jurifdictions in Scotland were annexed to the Crown.

The keeper of the caftle of Thrieff received from each of the twenty-fix or twenty-feven parifhes in the ftewarty of Kirkcudbright, what was called a ladner-mart cow, that is, a fat cow, in fuch condition as to be fit for killing and falting at Martinmas for winter provifion. Thefe ladner-mart cows were regularly paid to the Earls of Nithfdale, till the forfei-

ture

GALLOWAY.

ure of the laſt Earl in 1715, when it went into difuſe; but formerly, ſo attentive were the family to that right, that when, in the year 1704, they ſold the eſtate, upon which the caſtle of Thrieff ſtood, they reſerved the iſland and caſtle, that it might afford them a title to the twenty-ſeven ladner-mart cows belonging to the caſtle; and they regularly, by a written commiſſion, appointed a captain of the caſtle of Thrieff. This ruin is now ſaid to be the property of the Laird of Kelton; by what means it became private property I have not been able to learn; the Lords Maxwell appear to have held it only as tenants by a leaſe from the Crown.

This caſtle conſiſts of a large ſquare tower, built with a ſmall ſlate-like ſtone; is ſurrounded at a ſmall diſtance by an envelope, with four round towers; it had alſo a ſtrong gate, ſhewn in the drawing; the curtains of the envelope were pierced for guns.

During the troubles under King Charles I. the Earl of Nithſdale held this caſtle for the King, and armed, paid, and victualled, a garriſon therein of eighty men, beſides officers, all at his own expence; till at length His Majeſty, unable to give him any aſſiſtance, directed and authoriſed him, by the following letters, to make the beſt conditions he could for himſelf and the garriſon of this caſtle, and alſo for that of Carleverock, wherein he had been for a conſiderable time beſieged.

Letter of King Charles I., addreſſed to our right truſty and right well-beloved couſin and counſellor, Robert, Earl of Nithſdale.

" Charles R.

" Right truſty and right well-beloved coſen and councellor, we greet you well. Whereas you have repreſented unto us, by your letter of the 12th of September, that thoſe who have beſieged you ſo long in the caſtle of Carlaverock have now offered you honourable conditions to come out; and foraſmuch as our affairs permit not to relieve you ſo ſoon as we had determined, and as ſeemes your neceſſities require, and being withal moſt willing to free your perſon from further danger, and to eaſe you of the trouble and toyle you have ſuſtained by ſo long a ſiege, we do therefore hereby (graciouſly condeſcending unto your humble requeſt) give you leave to embrace and accept the

aforeſaid

aforesaid conditions, for the safety and preservation of your person and estate, having withal a regard to our honour, so far as the necessity of your present condition will permit; and we shall still, as we have done hitherto, continue our gracious esteem of you. Given at our Court at York this 15th day of September, in the sixteenth year of our reign, 1640."

Letter from King Charles I., addressed as before.

" CHARLES R.

" RIGHT trusty and well-beloved cousen and counsellor, we greet you well. Understanding by this bearer, that altho' you were agreed with those that have beleaguered you in Carlaverock upon honourable terms, for your coming forth, and rendering thereof, yet that those conditions are not valid until such time that they be ratified by those that have made themselves members of the great Committee in Edinburgh, and fearing that your enemies there will not give way to your coming forth upon such good terms, we are therefore graciously pleased, and by these presents do permit and give you leave to take such conditions as you can get, whereby the lives and liberties of yourself, your family, and those that are with you, may be preserved: and in case they should urge the surrendry of our castle of Thrieve, which hitherto you have so well defended, and we wish you were able to do so still, our gracious pleasure is, that you do rather quit the same unto them; which, if so, the necessity require you to do on the best and most honourable terms you can, rather than hazard the safety of your own person, and those with you; and in such case this shall be your warrant and discharge. Given at our Court at York, the 15th day of September, in the sixteenth year of our reign, 1640."—This view was drawn A. D. 1789.

NEW ABBEY. PLATE I.

THIS was a Cistertian abbey, founded in the beginning of the thirteenth century by Devorgilla, daughter of Allan, Lord of Galloway, niece to David, Earl of Huntingdon, and wife to John Baliol, Lord of
Castle-

Castlebernard. Baliol died in the year 1269, and was buried in this new foundation.

ANDREW WINTON, prior of Lochlevin, informs us, that the lady, Devorgilla, caused his heart to be taken out and embalmed; and putting it into an ivory box, bound with enamelled silver, closed it solemnly in the walls of the church, near the high altar, from whence it was occasionally stiled the Abbey of Sweetheart, though afterwards more generally called New Abbey.

To this abbey there belonged divers baronies, lands, churches, and other valuable possessions, to the annual amount, in money, of 682 l. The particulars of some of these lands see in the note *.

---

* The kirks of St. Katherine, of the Hopes, Mont Lothian, Bolton, Kenniel Dorstorphin, Kirkpatrick, Durham, Corse Michael and Buitle, with the tiends of the same, all belonged to this abbey, together with the barony of Lochpatrick, comprehending the 49 merks, and 2 shilling lands, of old extent, of Kirkpatrick Durham, viz.

The 40 shilling land of Culshengan	
Ditto - - of Tarbreach	The 5 merk land of Atkinhay
The 20 shilling land of Kirkland	
The 40 shilling land of Monidow	The 1 merk land of Darngarroch
The 36 shilling land and eight-penny land of Bardarrock	The 40 shilling land of Calfat
Ditto - - of Nether Macartna	Ditto - - of Barmossete
The 20 shilling land of Margley	
The 40 shilling land of Craigileay	Ditto - - of Knocktulloch
Ditto - - of Arkland	
Ditto - - of Armone	The two merk land of Overbar.
Ditto - - of Drumconchre	

The 2 merk land of Netherbar, with the lands of Corse and Barbain, which are said to be pendicle of Bardarrock, and the mill, with all other and singular annexes, connexes, woods, fishings, parts, pendicles, and pertinents, &c., lying within the stewartry of Kirkcudbright, and shire of Dumfries; which lands were fewed 117 merks, 8 shillings, and 8 pennies, Scots, to Robert, Master of Maxwell, son and heir of Robert Lord Maxwell, to him and the heirs male of his body; which failing, to his brother John, and his heirs male; which failing, to the heirs male whatsoever, of the above-mentioned Robert, Master of Maxwell, for services done to the abbey by the family of Maxwell, for taking the abbey and tenants, &c. under their protection, as appears by the charter granted to him by John, abbot of the monastery of Sweetheart, and the convent of the same, bearing date February 18, 1544. The lands of Ardevell, Engleston, Corse Little Barr, Darngarrock, Kirkland of Corse Michael, Craigend and Leaths, belonged to this monastery, together with lands now belonging to William Craik, Esq. of Arbigland, and others.

THE first abbot of this house was Henry, who died in the journey to Citeaux, in the year 1219. He was succeeded by Ericus Magister, *converforum ejufdem domûs*; afterwards, according to Prynne, John, Abbot of this houfe, fwore fealty to Edward, furnamed Long Shanks, A. D. 1296, and was one of the free barons who chofe that King to be arbitrator between Bruce and Baliol.

FEBRUARY 18, A. D. 1548, the name of the incumbent abbot was John, as appears by his fignature to a charter to the Lords of Maxwell, then made heritable baillies of Sweetheart. This charter was alfo figned by 14 monks, whofe names were as under: 1. Richardus. 2. Thomas Pedden. 3. Jacobus Derling. 4. Frater Willielmus Johnstone. 5. Frater Gaven Little. 6. Frater Gilbertus Neilfon. 7. Frater Thomas Murray. 8. Frater Johannes Kirkpatrick. 9. Frater Robertus Notman. 10. Frater Patricius Welfh. 11. Frater Patricius Kowll. 12. Frater Andreas Donnart. 13. Frater Thomas Dickfon.

ON the 23d of October, A. D. 1558, one, named John, was abbot, as appears by a charter of his granting. Among the confenting monks, who figned the deed, is Gilbert Brown, of the family of Garfluth, who afterwards became abbot of this houfe, and was the laft that held that office. Calderwood, in his hiftory, fays, that he fat in Parliament on the 17th of Auguft, 1560, when the Confeffion of Faith was approved of; and, in 1605, was apprehended by the Lord Cranfton, captain of the guards appointed for the borders, and was fent firft to Blacknefs caftle, and, after fome days, to the caftle of Edinburgh, where he was confined till his departure out of the kingdom. He died at Paris the 14th of May, 1612.

AFTER the Reformation this abbey was in the hands of the Crown, from 1587, when the Annexation Act paffed, to the year 1624, when it was granted to Sir Robert Spotfwood of that ilk; in whofe time the yearly value of the barony was 212 l. 10s. 10½d. fterling. But it has fince been burdened by Queen Anne, with a mortification in favour of the fecond minifter of Dumfries, paid out of the lands of Drumm, in the parifh of New Abbey, which, with feveral decreets of locality, amount to 141 l. 4s. 8½d.

THIS abbey ftands in a bottom: the principal parts remaining, are the church

church and part of the chapter-houfe, faid to have been an elegant piece of architecture, demolifhed, as was reported, for the fake of the ftone. It was feared the whole building would have undergone the fame fate; wherefore a number of the neighbouring gentry raifed a fum of money by fubfcription, and the minifter was employed to enter into an agreement with the tenant to prevent it, for which forty pounds was paid him. It is but juftice to Mr. Copeland, the proprietor, who had purchafed this abbey of Mr. Spotfwood, to take notice that he had in his leafe prohibited and guarded againft all fuch dilapidations; but hurt that his neighbours fhould fuppofe him capable of fuch a piece of barbarifm as to permit fo great an ornament to the country to be demolifhed for the paltry fum of fix or feven pounds, the price he was faid to have gotten for the ftones, he, as a fine, or amende honourable to his character and tafte, permitted his tenant to take the fum above-mentioned. The minifters and fubfcribers are, however, juftly entitled to the thanks of the country for their public-fpirited behaviour on this occafion.

In the roof of the fouth tranfept is an efcutcheon, charged with two paftoral ftaves in faltire; over them a heart, and beneath them three mullets of five points, 2 and 1, faid to be the arms of the abbey; over the efcutcheon is an infcription, from its height, and want of light, illegible; it is faid to be, *Chriftus Maritus Meus*, which feems more applicable to a nunnery than a houfe of monks.

Meafures of this ruin, as communicated by Dr. Clapperton:

Area of the whole demefnes of this abbey, 16 acres.
Height of the tower, 90 feet.
Length of the whole church, 200 feet.
Breadth of the middle aifle, 25 feet.
Breadth of the fide aifles, 15 feet.
Tranfept, 102 feet.
Breadth of the arches, 15 feet.
Diameter of the columns at the bafe, 4 and ½ feet.
Height of the fhafts of the columns from bafe to capital, 10 feet.
N. B. Six in number.

Bafe

Bafe of the columns fupporting the tower, 10 feet.

Height of the fhafts of the columns fupporting the tower, 20 fet

THE parifh kirk ftands on the fouth fide of the church, and is formed out of part of the ruins; near it is a fmall gate leading into the abbey, on which is a bell—this is of a fingular ftile of architecture; on it are feveral defaced carvings in baffo relievo, with two efcutcheons of arms.

THE burial ground lies to the eaft of the abbey church; in it are fome ancient tombftones: on one a crofs, with a large and broad fword on the finifter fide of it.

THIS view was drawn A. D. 1789.

NEW ABBEY. PLATE II.

THE former view fhewed the north-weft appearance of this venerable ruin. This was taken a little to the eaftward of the fouth.

BUTEL CASTLE.

THIS ruin was the baronial caftle of Butel, built out of the materials of a very ancient caftle of the fame name. It ftands in the ftewartry of Kirkcudbright, in Galloway, and parifh of Butel, on the weft fide of the water of Urr, about fifteen miles from Dumfries to the weftward, and is now the property of George Maxwell, of Muncies, Efq.

THE ancient building, from whofe remains this was erected, ftood at a very fmall diftance. The mount, fome fcattered fragments of walls, a draw-well, and the furrounding fofs, all overgrown with trees, fhrubs, and bufhes, are the fole remains of this fortrefs, faid to have been confiderable when Galloway was an independent ftate, and afterwards to have been the favourite refidence of John Baliol, fometime King of Scotland.

THIS view was drawn A. D. 1789.

THE

ABBOT'S HOUSE.

GALLOWAY.

THE ABBOT'S TOWER, NEAR NEW ABBEY.

This tower was the refidence of the abbots of Sweetheart, or New Abbey, when they chofe to retire for a fhort time from the cares of their office. It commands an extenfive profpect, and, when in repair, muft have been a very healthy habitation, much more fo than the abbey, which lies rather low.

In perufing Keith's lift of churchmen, it will appear that Sweetheart Abbey produced fome eminent ftatefmen and divines, who, it is probable, here planned their political fyftem, or purfued their facred refearches, free from the forms, duties, and intrigues of the convent; for all focieties, even convents, have their intrigues.

This place is now the property of Mrs. Maxwell, of Kirkconnell, who purchafed it fome years ago.

This view was drawn A. D. 1789.

THE MOTE OF URR. Plate I.

This artificial mount was, according to tradition, what is implied by the Saxon term, *mote*, that is, a place of judicature, or public affembly; and when Galloway was an independent ftate, this was the court where the Reguli, or petty Kings of that diftrict, held their national councils, and promulgated fuch new laws and regulations as were found neceffary from time to time to be enacted. It was alfo the feat of judgment, where their doomfters or judges tried capital offenders. At this time Galloway was divided into two diftricts, namely, above and below the water of Cree. The mote of Urr was then the great court of judicature for the latter. This mount, or hill, greatly refembles that of the Tinewald, in the Ifle of Man, which is appropriated to the fame ufes.

This kind of court was not peculiar to Galloway, or the Ifle of Man. Mounts called motes, and court hills, are to be feen near a great number of caftles and baronial manfions, not only in Scotland, but in England alfo: their ufe, however, as courts of juftice, feems forgotten

forgotten in England, where it has been generally fuppofed that they were conftructed for military purpofes, particularly to anfwer the ufes of cavaliers, in overlooking or commanding the moveable towers, or other works of an enemy.

MOTE OF URR. Plate II.

The mote of Urr is here fhown from a different point of view, whence its form may be better diftinguifhed than in the former plate, where it is fomewhat fubdued by the intervening trees and houfes.

Both thefe views were drawn A. D. 1789.

DUNDRENNAN ABBEY. Plate I.

The following account of the foundation of this abbey is chiefly tranfcribed from the Appendix to Keith's Catalogue of the Bifhops, &c.

" Dundrennan Abbey, fituate on Solway Frith, about two miles from Kirkcudbright, in Galloway, was founded by Fergus, Lord of Galloway, in the year 1142. The monks thereof were of the Ciftertian order, brought from Rievall, in England. Sylvanus was the firft abbot of this place; he died at Belleland, 7 mo. Id. Octobris, anno 1189. The laft abbot hereof was Edward Maxwell, fon to John Lord Herries, after whofe death King James VI. annexed, this place to his royal chapel of Sterling. The chronicle of Melrofs is thought to have been written by an abbot of this monaftery. The firft part thereof is certainly penned by an Englifhman, and is a continuation of Bede's Hiftory; the fecond part appears to have been written by a Scotfman, familiar and contemporary with our Stuarts. The Oxford edition, publifhed in the year 1684, does not agree with our manufcripts. Alan, Lord of Galloway, was buried in this place in the year 1233." In the Appendix to Keith's Hiftory of the Church and ftate of Scotland, the annual revenues of this houfe, in money, is faid to amount to 500l.

This monaftery, as is evident from its ruins, was once both a beautiful

ful and extensive pile, but is now miserably dilapidated. Hither the unfortunate Queen Mary was escorted from Terreagles by the Lord Herries, and from hence she is said to have set out for England.

The tomb of Alan, Lord of Galloway, was lately to be seen; he lay in a niche in the cross aisle, on the east side of the north door. It is now demolished, but the mutilated trunk of his effigy is still shewn; he was represented in a recumbent posture, and cross-legged like a crusader; for though the figure is deprived of its legs, the position of the thighs shew they were crossed. He is habited in mail armour, over which is a surcoat, a belt cross his right shoulder, and another round his waist. His lady, it is said, lay on the other side of the door.

From a plan, in the possession of the minister, it appears that the church of this monastery was in the shape of a cross; that over the intersection of the body and the transept there was a spire, which, tradition says, was 200 feet high. The body was 120 feet in length, and divided into three aisles by seven clustered columns supporting arches on each side. The breadth of the side aisles was 15 feet each, that of the middle aisle 25 feet. The transept measured, from north to south, 120 feet, from east to west 46 feet.

The east end of the church was of the same breadth as the middle aisle, and only 35 feet in length; four small clustered columns, raning on each side of, and in a line with, the two easternmost that supported the spire, divide the transept into two unequal portions.

On the south side of the church were the cloysters, containing a square area of 94 feet, with a grass-plat in the center; east and west, but chiefly south of the cloysters, were the lodgings and different offices of the monastery, occupying a space of near 200 feet square; to- towards the south end of the western side of these buildings was a small projecting erection, in shape of a cross, exactly similar to the church, but inverted, those parts which fronted the east in one, facing the west in the other.

This view, which shews the north transept of the church, and the adjoining offices of the monastery, as viewed from the north-west, was drawn A. D. 1789.

DUNDRENNAN ABBEY. Plate II.

This view shews the eastern aspect of the building, which now belongs to Thomas Carnes, Esq. of London, who purchased it about two years ago of the family of —— Curry, Esq.

GLENLUCE ABBEY. Plate I.

GLENLUCE, or Vallis lucis, in Galloway, gives name to a considerable Bay, as well as this Abbey, which was of the Ciftertain order, founded in the year 1190 by Rolland, Lord of Galloway, and Constable of Scotland.

The monks of this monastery were brought from Melrofs. Walter, abbot of this place, was sent to Scotland by John, duke of Albany. Laurence Gordon, son to Alexander, bishop of Galloway, and archbishop of Athens, was likewise an abbot of this place. King James VI. in the year 1602, erected Glenluce into a temporality, which, in 1606, was confirmed by an act of parliament. After his death, John Gordon, dean of Salisbury, son to the bishop above-mentioned, became Lord Glenluce, and disposed of the lordship to Sir Robert Gordon, his son-in-law. Afterwards Glenluce was united to the bishopric of Galloway by act of parliament, and at length Sir James Dalrymple, president of the session, a gentleman of an ancient family in Carrick, was created Lord Glenluce; his son, Sir James Dalrymple, king's advocate, justice clerk, and secretary of state, was likewise Lord Glenluce and Earl of Stair.

AMONG Mr. M'Farlan's papers, in the Advocate's library, Edinburgh, is a description of Galloway by Mr. Andrew Sympson, A. D. 1684, wherein the ruins of this abbey are thus described:—" In this parish, that is Glenluce, about half a mile or more northward from the parock kirke, is the abbey of Glenluce, situated in a very pleasant valley, on the east side of the river of Luce: the steeple, and part of the walls of the church, together with the chapter-house, the walls of the cloyster, the gatehouse, with the walls of the large precincts, are for the most part yet standing. In this parish of Glenluce there was a spirit, which for a long time molested the house of one Campbell,

Glenluce Abbey. Pl. I.

GALLOWAY.

bell, a weaver: it would be tedious to give a full relation of all the stories concerning it. Sinclair, in his Hydrostatics, gives some account of it."

Of the abbey of Glenluce the present remains consist of the chapter-house, which is still covered, some adjoining vaults, and two high gables of the western part of the church. The chapter-house and vaults have handsome windows, of pointed arches, divided by two mullions, the heads of the windows adorned with tracery; the chapter-house, which is a square of about 28 feet, was adorned with sculpture, but neither very elegantly designed nor executed. In the ceiling, at the intersection of the arches, are two coats of arms, one within a tressure, a lion rampant, a coronet over the shield, which appears to be supported by angels; the other a lion rampant crowned; a bracket supporting an arch, has a man's head, with a scroll beneath it, on which was an inscription, but for want of light it was illegible. The jaumbs of the door are also carved; on one is a man's head, on the other some foliage.

The chapter-house opens into a little garden on the south, round which there seems to have been a cloister; some of the walls have marks of the insertion of joists.

This ruin has been greatly defaced for the sake of its stone, for building houses and walls. A storm, likewise, some few years ago, threw down a high gable of the church.

The manse, or minister's house, stands on part of the site of the abbey. The ruins are now the property of Sir Thomas Hay, of Park.

This view was drawn A. D. 1789.

GLENLUCE ABBEY. Plate II.

This view was taken from a station a little to the right of that from whence the former plate was drawn, in order to open the gable end of the church.

LOCH ROIETON, OR THE HILLS CASTLE.

This castle takes its first name from an adjacent lough; it is situated about three miles south-west from Dumfries. The present building,

building, from its ftile, does not feem older than the middle of the fixteenth century; indeed, from the dates of 1598 and 1600 over the gate and inner court, it is moft likely fome re-edification, or great repair, took place in thofe times.

From the wardrobe account of the year 1300, publifhed by the fociety of Antiquaries, it appears here was at the time a caftle or manfion, of fufficient fize and confequence to receive King Edward I. who remained here one night, in his way from the caftle of Caerleverock to Kirkcudbright, and in his chapel here offered up his oblations: the words of the original are, " 17 die Julii in Oblac' Regis ad Altare in Capella fua upud Loghroieton 7s." Poffibly the royal chapel might have been a tent or portable building.

THIS fortalice was afterwards one of the ftrengths poffeffed by the Douglas family, when Lords of Galloway, and upon the ruin of that houfe was granted to the Herries family, from whom it came to the Lords Maxwell, and devolved to a cadet of that houfe, thence denominated Maxwell of the Hills, according to a copy of an ancient pedigree of the Nithfdale family in the poffeffion of captain Robert Riddel, of Friars Carfe, F. A. S. Robert the fon of the fixth Lord Maxwell, by Beatrix, the daughter of James, Earl of Morton, died here September 13th, 1552, aged about five years, having furvived Lord Robert, his father, only a year. This infant, Robert, is not mentioned in Douglas Peerage; his brother John there ftands as the immediate fucceffor to Lord Robert; by this family the caftle and its demefnes were fold, and are at prefent the property of —— M'Culluck, of Ardwall, Efq.

THIS edifice, which furrounds a fquare court, is now divided into different tenements. Several coats of arms, with initial letters, are fet up on different parts of the buildings, chiefly thofe of the Maxwells and their alliances; over the gate, which is pierced with loopholes for mufquetry, are the arms of Scotland, and the date 1598. There is another efcutcheon, the date 1600; both, probably, commemorating, as has been before obferved, the times of fome confiderable repairs or erection.

THIS view was drawn A. D. 1789.

KIRKCUDBBRIGHT CASTLE. PLATE I.

HERE was an ancient caftle belonging to the Dowals, Lords of Galloway, when Galloway was a regality independent of the kingdom of Scotland. This caftle defcended with the other property of the Lords of Galloway, to Dervorgelda, heirefs of Allan, the laft Lord of that regality, and was afterwards annexed to the crown, till James IV. by a charter, dated at Edinburgh, 26th of February, 1509, granted it, together with the caftle mains, to the Burgh of Kirkcudbright. The mounds and dykes of this caftle are ftill remaining; by its fituation it evidently appears to have been conftructed to defend the entrance of the river Dee.

IN the town of Kirkcudbright, and probably in this caftle, King Edward I. refided fome days, when on his expedition to the fiege of Carleverock, in the year 1300, as is fhewn in the wardrobe account of that year, lately publifhed by the Society of Antiquaries of London.

KIRKCUDBRIGHT CASTLE alfo afforded a temporary refuge to the unfortunate King Henry VI. after the battle of Towton, as may be feen in the Pafton Letters, vol. I. p. 248, wherein is the following paffage, " The Kyng Herry is at Kirkowbre with iiij men and a childe, Quene Margaret is at Edinburgh and hir fon;" this is at the bottom of a copy of a letter, dated at Diepe, 30th of Auguft, 1461.

KING JAMES IV. of Scotland was at Kirkcudbright in March, 1508, as is proved by public papers, dated at that place. The tradition is, that he was hofpitably entertained there, and that the burgh claimed a reward for their former fervices to James II. and to himfelf, whereupon he, with confent of parliament, granted them the old caftle and mains, as has been above-mentioned.

THE latter caftle of Kirkcudbright, here delineated, was built by Thomas M·Lellan of Bombay, anceftor of the Lords of Kirkcudbright, about the year 1570, on the fite of the collegiate church, then lately demolifhed by the reformers, which was granted by King James VI. then a minor, the earl of Murray being the regent. This charter

conveyed

conveyed the whole and entire fite,* foundation, and place, upon which the place and church of the brothers of Kirkcudbright, were originally conftructed or erected, together with ftones therein remaining, with all the orchards, gardens, and appurtenances." It was dated 6th December, 1569. The defcendants of this Sir Thomas enjoyed the caftle he had built till April 1663, when fome women, having made a difturbance at the introduction of an epifcopal minifter into the Kirk of Kirkcudbright, the privy council granted a commiffion to the Earls of Linlithgow, Galloway, Annandale, and Drumlanrig, with Sir John Wauchop, to enquire into the matter. Thefe four earls came to Kirkcudbright caftle, and found that Lord Kirkcudbright had countenanced what thofe women had done; they therefore fent him prifoner to Edinburgh, 23d May, 1663, where he fhortly after died, and his neighbours by degrees acquired all his eftates.

During the Ufurpation of Cromwell, this lord, with moft of the Scotch Prefbyterians, had oppofed the independents, by which he had fuffered greatly in his fortune; but being likewife a great opponent to epifcopacy, he became obnoxious to government.

After his death the caftle of Kirkcudbright came at length by fucceffion to the late Sir Robert Maxwell, of Orchardton; he fold it to the prefent Earl of Selkirk, who is the prefent proprietor.

The remains of this building fhew it was once an elegant as well as large ftructure; fome ancient perfons living when this view was taken, faid, that it had extended much farther than it then did, had formerly a handfome gate, and that the roof was taken off about forty years ago, fince which it has been much injured, the ftones having been taken for other erections.

Against the building are two coats of arms; over that on the finifter fide are the initials, G M, and the date, 1582, probably the time when the caftle was completed, or fome confiderable addition made to it. The arms are thofe of Herries, the Three Hedgehogs,

---

* Totum et integrum folum fundum et locum, fuper quibus locus et ecclefiæ Fratrum de Kirkcudbright per prius conftrucbantur feu ædificabantur, una cum omnibus lapidibus fuper cifdem exiftentibus, cum pomariis, hortis et pendiculis.

this

beneath them this motto, DONS DEDIT, and another obliterated inscription, which, according to tradition, was, This is the Houfe of Herries.

KIRKCUDBRIGHT CASTLE. PLATE II.

This view fhews the North afpect; the former was taken from the Eaft: both were drawn A. D. 1789.

KENMURE CASTLE. PLATE I.

This caftle ftands on a very commanding eminence, at the head of Loch Ken, where the water of the Ken runs into the lake. It is faid to have been one of the feats of the ancient Lords of Galloway, and particularly the favourite refidence of John Baliol, fome time King of Scotland.

KENMURE was for a fhort time in the hands of the Douglases, and afterwards, A. D. 1297, with the lands of Lochinvar, acquired from John de Maxwell, by Sir Adam de Gordon, Knight, and has ever fince continued in his family, one of whom, Sir John Gordon, of Lochinvar, was (according to Douglas) by King Charles I. raifed on the 8th of May, 1633, to the dignity of the Peerage, by the titles of Vifcount Kenmure, Lord Lochinvar, to him and his heirs male; and as a farther teftimony of his majefty's favor, part of his lands were erected into a royal borough, with ample jurifdiction, to be called the Burgh of Galloway, now New Galloway, with which Wigton, Whithorn, and Stranraur, fends a member to the Britifh parliament.

ROBERT, the feventh Vifcount, from a too grateful fenfe of the favors conferred on his anceftors by the Stuart family, unhappily engaging in the Rebellion, A. D. 1715, was taken prifoner at Prefton, tried, condemned, and executed: his honors and moft of his eftates confequently forfeited to the crown. Since which his defcendants have, by their fervices in the army, endeavoured to compenfate for the miftaken attachment of their predeceffor.

THE buildings of this castle consist chiefly of two towers, now in ruins, to which some later erections, still habitable, have been added, encompassing a square court. Tradition says, this castle has been twice burned: once during the reign of Queen Mary, and a second time by Oliver Cromwell, or his order. In digging lately near the foot of the mount on which the castle stands, a great number of cannon balls were discovered, some forty-eight, and others six-pounders.

THIS plate, which shews the distant view of the castle, the lake, and romantic mountains rising behind it, was drawn A. D. 1790.

KENMURE CASTLE. PLATE II.

THIS plate, which shews the entrance into the castle, was drawn at the same time as plate I.

THE LAGGAN STONE. PLATE I.

THIS huge stone, which is so poised as to be moveable with a small exertion of force, stands near the summit of a high ridge of mountains, called the Kells Rins. The particular hill on which it is situated is called Mullæ, and the stone itself is called the Mickle Lump; near it is a small pool of water which covers about half a rood of land. The dimensions of this stone are, its greatest length eight feet nine inches, its height five feet one inch and a half, its circumference twenty-two feet nine inches.

THIS plate gives the appearance of the stone as seen at a small distance; the figure serves as a scale to determine its magnitude.

THE LAGGAN STONE. PLATE II.

A DISTANT view of this stone is here exhibited, with the adjacent rocks. Both views were drawn A. D. 1790.

IT

LAGGAN STONE PH.

Lagan Stone Pit.

It seems doubtful whether most of these rocking stones are the effect of art or chance. Some suppose them to have been thus poised by the Druids, with an intention to impose on their followers by the appearance of a miracle; others think them the product of accident, on stones of a particular form, the circumjacent earth being washed from their bases by some torrent or heavy rain.

CASTLE KENNEDY.

Wigtonshire.

This castle stands in an island well planted with trees, in a beautiful lough. The exact time of its construction is not known; but probably it was not built till after the year 1668, as it is not mentioned in a charter or retour of that date. This view was taken A. D. 1789, from the high road leading from Newton Stewart to Stranrawer.

Castle Kennedy was anciently the seat of the Cassillis family, from one of whom it was purchased by the first Earl of Stair. The ruinous state of the part here shewn, was occasioned by an accidental fire, which happened in 1717, and is supposed to have begun in the laundry. Every thing was consumed, but no lives were lost, as the family were not at home: the gardener saved himself by jumping out of a high window.

DUNSKEY CASTLE.

Dunskey Castle stands about half a mile south of Port Patrick, on the neck of a rocky cliff which projects out into the sea at the extremity of the Mull of Galloway. The building occupies the whole front or breadth, but has an æra or parade behind it, about twenty yards deep; it was vaulted, and seems to have been calculated for defence; the access to it was over a draw-bridge. In the back parts of the castle there are some remains of ornaments,

which

which shew it was once a handsome building; many of the squared stones have been taken away by the owner, for the purpose of building a modern seat; the rooms were most of them very small; the stair-case was in the east angle.

History mentions a castle here as early as the time of Eugen V. who began his reign A. D. 685. In that king's reign it is said to have been besieged by Egfrid, King of Bernicia. It is also said by Mr. Andrew Sympson to have been once a great castle belonging to the Lords of Airds, in Ireland; both these relations must certainly refer to some former castle or castles on or near the same spot; for, from the stile of the present building, it is evidently apparent that it is not older than the middle of the sixteenth century, nor is it entitled to the epithet of large; it is, nevertheless, strongly situated with respect to the sea, though commanded from a variety of places on the land side: when Mr. Sympson wrote, it belonged to John Blair, of Dunskey, son and heir of master John Blair, late minister of Portpatrik; it is at present the property of the representative of Sir James Hunter Blair, who married the heiress, and has an elegant modern house in the neighbourhood. This castle, like many other ancient buildings, lies under the report of being haunted with evil spirits; and it is particularly affirmed that a minister of the parish had here a bickering with the foul fiend Satan himself, whom he put to flight.

DUNSKEY CASTLE. Plate I.

This plate shews a nearer view of the castle, as it appears from a station almost opposite to that from whence the former drawing was made. Both were taken A. D. 1789.

AYRSHIRE.

THE COLLEGIATE CHURCH OF MAYBOLE, OR MINIBOIL.

This collegiate church was founded in the year 1441, by Sir Gilbert Kennedy, of Dinnure, anceftor to the Earl of Caffils, for a provoft or rector, and feveral prebendaries: it was confecrated in honour of the blefled Virgin Mary. The founder, by his charter, dated at Edinburgh, the 18th of May, in the year before-mentioned, endowed it with all, and fingular, his lands of Largenlen and Brocklack, within the county of Carrick.

In a manufcript defcription of Carrick, by the Reverend Mr. Abercrombie, minifter of Miniboile, among Mr. M'Farlan's collection, there is the following defcription of this place. "There was alfo a collegiate church at Mayboll, the fabric whereof is ftill extant and entyre, being now ufed as the burial place of the Earls of Caffillis, and other gentlemen, who contributed to the putting a roofe upon it when it was decayed. On the north fide of which kirk is the buriall place of the Lord of Colaine; within are two enclofures of new fquare ftone, lately built; the college confifted of a rector and three prebends, whofe ftalls are all of them yet extant, fave the rector's, which was where thofe low buildings and the garden are, on the eaft fide of that which is now the parfon's houfe, with the orchard and the wall-trees. The patrimony of this church, were the provofts and priefts lands, in the parifh of Kirk Michael, which fell into the Earl of Caffillis's hands, upon the diffolution of the college at the reformation, out of which he as yet payes yearly to the minifter of Mayboll, the fum of 70 marks Scots. As for the church its prefent patrimony is out of the tyth of the parifh, which before the reformation, was all poffeffed and enjoyed by the nuns of North Berwick, and on the diffolution of the faid nunnerie, became a prize to the Laird of Bergeney. The parifh church ftands at a little diftance from the forefaid college, eaftward; it does not appear when it was built, but the large ifle that lies from the body of the church, fouthward, and makes the figure of the church a T, was built by Mr. James Bonar, minifter thereat, in the reign of K. Charles the Firft. Within the faid parifh of Mayboll, there have been other chappels of old, as Kirkbride, on the coaft fide, whofe walls and yard be yet extant; and within the lands of Achindrain, and elfewhere, there have been other chappels, whereof the rudera are yet to be feen.

The towne of Mayboll ftands on an afcending ground from eaft to weft, and lies open to the fouth; it hath one principal ftreet declining towards the eaft; it is pretty well fenced from the north by a higher ridge of hills that lies above it, at a fmall diftance northwards; it hath one principal ftreet, with houfes on both fides, built of free ftone; and it is beautified with the fituation of two caftles, one at each end of this ftreet; that to the eaft belongs to the Earl of Caffillis, beyond which, caftward, ftands a great new building, which be his granaries. On the weft end is a caftle, which belonged to the Laird of Blarrquhan, which is now the Tolbuith, and is adorned with a pyramide, and a row of bullufters round it, raifed upon the top of the ftair-cafe, into which they have mounted a fyne clock."

This view was drawn 1789.

ST. JOHN THE BAPTIST'S CHURCH, AYR.

For the following account of this building I am indebted to a reverend gentleman, whofe name I am not authorifed to mention. The ruins of the church of St. John the Baptift, ftands between the town and the fea, within the fort, built by Oliver Cromwell: it is faid to have been entire about fixty years ago; at prefent the tower only remains: it foundation may ftill be traced, from which it appears to have been in the form of a crofs. Among the archives of this town, is
a charter

St. John Baptist Church.

a charter from Robert II. furnamed the Blear-eyed, A. D. 1378, refpecting the preferving this church from being deftroyed by the blowing of fand;* but the church has, it is faid, been fince quite demolifhed through want of tafte, and the guilt of avarice; though there is evidence of its having been the feat of a parliament, held in the time of Bruce and Baliol, and where a number of the nobility and gentry determined upon noble and free motives, for the former: a copy

---

* Coppie of King Robert his charter to the burgh of Air, allowing a gratification to thofe who fhould preferve the burgh and church from being deftroyed with fand. Robertus Dei gratia Rex Scotorum, omnibus probis hominibus totius terræ, feu Clericis, vel Laicis falutem, Dum Burgus nofter de Air, per motionem & agitationem arenæ fit quafi totaliter annihilatus & deftructus, et . . . . . . fimiliter per brevis proceffum temporis ad finalem deftructionem redegi videbitur, nifi citius per difcretorum virorum folertia et diligentia remedium apponitur; nos igitur defiderantes de Aliquo . . . . . competente in hac parte futuro providere, et precipue caufa ecclefiæ Johannes Baptifti quam in honore, reverentia et devotione femper intendebam et intendam mantinere, protegere et fovere, cujus cæmeterium per violentiam motionis arenæ ut predicitur fere utiq. ad fundamentum ipfius ecclefiæ adeo eft denudata et deftructa quod multorum offa defunctorum ibidem humata, videntur per ventorum violentiam de terra evulfa penitus et circa. Conceffimus de gratia noftra fpeciali illis quicunque fuerint, qui in hac parte defenfionem appofuerunt, et ipfam villam, ecclefiam ei cæmeterium a deftructione dicta arenæ liberaverint, omnes pacatas vaftus infra dictum burgum quos meditantibus illorum laboribus et impenfis a deftructione præfata arenofa liberaverint, et fuerint habitabiles, tenendas et habendas eifdem dicturam pacatarum prænominatis.

Conqueftoribus et hæredibus fuis de nobis et hæredibus noftris in feudo et hereditate in libero burgagio, libere et quiete pleniarie integre et honorifice, reddendo inde annuatim de qualibet pacato predicto, poftquam effecte fuerint habitabiles aut habitabilis, unum denarium fterlinenfem ad feftem Penticoftis, tum pro omnia ferme inde exegenda aut folvenda. In cujus rei teftimonium præfenti Chartæ noftræ, noftrum præcipimus apponi figellum, teftibus veretabilibus in Chrifto patribus Willielmo et Joanne Cancellariis noftris St. Andreæ et Dunkelden Ecclefiarum Epifcopis, Joanne primoprogenito noftro de Carick feu Scotia, Roberto de Fyffe et de Monteith de filio noftro dilecto Willielmo de Douglas et de Marr, confanguineo noftro comitibus Jacobo Lindefay nepote noftro Kentigerno et Alexandro de Lindefay, confanguineo noftro militibus apud Edenburgum decimo die Decembris Anno Regni noftro Anno decimo. After the copy of this charter, the tranfcriber adds the following note. " I find this to have been granted by Robert the fecond, furnamed Bleird eye; for John was his eldeft fon, by Elizabeth Muir, and Robert of Fyfe and Monteith his other fon of that marriage. Robert the fecond's reign commenced in the year 1368; and he died in the nineteenth year of his reign; fo that by calculation this charter had been granted in the year 1378."

of their names and fignatures is ftill extant, many of them could not write. Tradition fays, that Comwell having taken in this church in order to erect a fort, gave the town a thoufand Englifh marks to build another. This feems probable from the minutes of the town council, at a community meeting, the 3d of July 1652. " Anent the fituation of building of the kirk all condefcend tall poffible meanes be ufed for building the fame, either upon Sewalton's ground, or the Grey Friars; and that the fame be bought; and that the town be ftented for als much as to utfit the fame, what is deficient of the money to be had frae the Englifh." The new kirk appears to have been built 1654.

In 1789, when this view was drawn, the tower of the church was very entire; feveral modern tomb-ftones were ftanding about it, from whence it fhould feem as if it were ftill ufed as a place of burial.

The fort above-mentioned, built by Oliver Cromwell, is a parallelogram, the greateft length from North to South defended by fix baftions; there are alfo two or three magazines, feemingly meant for bomb proof, one of them ferves for a gate, which is here fhewn in the drawing. It was by King Charles II. granted to Lord Eglington; the property is now in his lady, who mortgaged it to the Lord Caffilis for 1000l. Several perfons now living remember moft of the walls ftanding.

DUNURE CASTLE. Plate I.

D<small>UNURE</small> C<small>ASTLE</small> is a fine old building, moft romantickly fituated on the brink of a perpendicular rocky cliff, in fome parts over-hanging the fea; beneath it is a cavern, called the Browney's Cave, now nearly filled up with rubbifh fallen from the rock and building: it is faid to have formerly communicated with the caftle, and probably ferved as a fally-port, or fecret communication with the fea; as in Dunbar and Turnbury caftle.

Nothing can exceed the fublimity of the profpect from this caftle, whence at one coup d'oeil is feen the conical rock of Lamlafh, and over it the craggy mountains of the Ifle of Arran, frequently hiding their heads in the clouds; from hence alfo may be feen the rock of Ailſa, the coaſt of Kentire, on both ſides of Arran, the coaſt of Ireland, the iſlands of Bute and Camreas, and a great part of the bay of Ayr.

By whom, or at what time this caſtle was built, I have not been able to learn; from its ſtrength and ſituation it muſt formerly have been of conſequence as a fortreſs.

DANURE CASTLE was an ancient reſidence of a principal branch of the Kennedy family, who were thence called Kennedy's of Dunure, and generally eſteemed the head of that name; the Caſſilis family is deſcended from it, and were proprietors of this eſtate till the beginning of the preſent century, when it was ſold to the grandfather of the preſent proprietor, alſo a deſcendant from the Kennedys of Dunure. It ſeems a matter of doubt, whether this caſtle has been inhabited ſince the reign of King James VI.

DUNURE CASTLE. PLATE II.

THE former view was taken from an eminence above the caſtle. This was drawn from the rocks on the ſhore beneath it, and ſhews the Weſt ſide of the keep, and its adjacent building.

BOTH views were taken A. D. 1789.

THE OLD HOUSE OF CASSILIS.

HERE is a great ſquare tower, whoſe walls are of an uncommon thickneſs, with a court of leſſer buildings, beautifully ſituated on a bank above the water of Dun, and ſurrounded by extenſive woods of old timber. This old tower is aſcended by a turnpike-ſtaircaſe; the lower ſtory is vaulted; the walls, as high as the third ſtory, are ſaid to be ſixteen feet thick. Here are many family portraits, and diverſe other paintings. This tower has probably undergone many repairs; the preſent appearance of the building does not beſpeak the laſt to be older than the reign of Queen Mary, or James VI. her ſon. This houſe belongs to the Earl of Caſſilis. The view was drawn A. D. 1789.

THE CASTLE OF DOLQUHARRAN.

In Mr. M'Farlan's collection, in the Advocate's library, Edinburgh, there is the following description of this castle: "The stately castle of Dolquharran, the building whereof is much improved, by the addition lately made thereto, which makes it by very far the best house in all that country, surrounded with vast inclosures of wood, that the country is not able to consume it, by their building and other instruments; and among them be oak trees of a considerable size, both for height and breadth, that will serve either for joist or roof of a good house." This castle at present consists of an old tower or fortalice, to which is joined a more modern house; probably the addition above-mentioned, from the figures over the door, was made in the year 1679. It is bounded by the garden on one side, and on the other by the water of Gervan. On the old tower are escutcheons of the arms of Kennedy, and another coat, seemingly that of Stewart, but much defaced by age; over the entrance are also some armorial bearings. From the battlements of the tower there is a fine prospect, the river winding under the eye, through a well-wooded valley. This venerable building is the property of Thomas Kennedy, of Dunure, Esq. for whom Mr. Adams is erecting a handsome house, of the castellated form, in the adjacent demesnes.

This view was drawn A. D. 1789.

GREENAND CASTLE

This view shews the castle of Grenand, as it appears on the road from Ayr to Maybole. The following description is given of this castle, in Mr. M'Farlan's MS. collection:

Castle of Grenand and the Cave. The Grenand is a high house upon the top of a rock hanging over upon the sea, with some lower new work, lately added to it, but never finished; it is too open to the cold and moisture arising from the sea to be a desirable habitation, and has been designed to be the owner's security against a surprize, rather than a constant residence. It is within the parish of Maybole.

This view was drawn A. D. 1789.

ALLO-

Alloa Church, Ayrshire.

ALLOWAY CHURCH,* AYRSHIRE.

THIS church stands by the river, a small distance from the bridge of Doon, on the road leading from Maybole to Ayr. About a century ago it was united to the parish of Ayr; since which time it has fallen

to

---

* This church is also famous for being the place wherein the witches and warlocks used to hold their infernal meetings, or sabbaths, and prepare their magical unctions; here too they used to amuse themselves with dancing to the pipes of the muckle-horned Deel. Diverse stories of these horrid rites are still current: one of which my worthy friend Mr. Burns has here favoured me with in verse.

TAM O' SHANTER. A TALE.

WHEN chapmen billies leave the street,
And drouthy neebors neebors meet,
As market-days are wearing late,
And folk begin to tak the gate;
While we sit bowsing at the nappy,
And gettin fou, and unco happy,
We think na on the long Scots miles,
The waters, mosses, slaps and styles,
That lie between us and our hame,
Where sits our sulky, sullen dame,
Gathering her brows, like gathering storm,
Nursing her wrath to keep it warm.

This truth fand honest Tam o'Shanter,
As he frae Ayr ae night did canter;
(Auld Ayr, whom ne'er a town surpasses
For honest men and bonnie lasses.)

O Tam! hadst thou but been sae wise
As taen thy ain wife Kate's advice!
She tauld thee weel, thou was a skellum,
A bletherin, blusterin, drunken blellum;
That frae November till October,
Ae market-day thou was na sober:
That ilka melder, wi' the miller,
Thou sat as long as thou had siller
That every naig was ca'd a shoe on,
The smith and thee gat roarin fou on:
That at the L—d's house, even on Sunday,
Thou drank wi' Kirkton Jean till Monday.
She prophesied that, late or soon,
Thou wad be found deep-drown'd in Doon;
Or catch'd wi' warlocks in the mirk
By Aloway's old haunted kirk.

Ah, gentle dames! it gars me greet,
To think how mony counsels sweet,
How mony lengthen'd sage advices,
The husband frae the wife despises!

But to our tale:—Ae market-night,
Tam had got planted unco right,
Fast by an ingle bleezing finely,
Wi' reamin swats that drank divinely;
And at his elbow, souter Johnie,
His ancient, truty, drouthy cronie;
Tam lo'ed him like a vera brither,
They had been fou for weeks tegither.—
The night drave on wi' sangs and clatter,
And ay the ale was growing better:
The landlady and Tam grew gracious,
With favours secret, sweet, and precious;
The souter tauld his queerest stories;
The landlord's laugh was ready chorus:
The storm without might rair and rustle,
Tam did na mind the storm a whistle.—
Care, mad to see a man sae happy,
E'en drown'd himself amang the nappy:
As bees flee hame, wi' lades o' treasure,
The minutes wing'd their way wi' pleasure.
Kings may be blest, but Tam was glorious,
O'er a' the ills o' life victorious!

But pleasures are like poppies spread,
You sieze the flower, its bloom is shed;
Or like the snow falls in the river,
A moment white—then melts for ever;
Or like the borealis race,
That flit ere you can point their place;

Or

to ruins. It is one of the eldest parishes in Scotland, and still retains these privileges: the minister of Ayr is obliged to marry and baptise in it, and also here to hold his parochial catechisings. The magistrates attempted,

---

Or like the rainbow's lovely form,
Evanishing amid the storm.—
Nae man can tether time or tide,
The hour approaches Tam maun ride;
That hour o'night's black arch the key stane,
That dreary hour he mounts his beast in;
And sic a night he takes the road in
As ne'er poor sinner was abroad in.

The wind blew, as 'twad blawn its last;
The rattling showers rose on the blast;
The speedy gleams the darkness swallow'd,
Loud, deep, and lang, the thunder bellow'd;
That night a child might understand
The deil had business on his hand,

Weel mounted on his grey meere, Meg,
A better never lifted leg,
Tam skelpit on thro' dub and mire,
Despising wind, and rain, and fire
Whyles holding fast his gude blue bonnet;
Whyles crooning o'er an auld Scots sonnet;
Whyles glowring round wi' prudent cares,
Lest bogles catch him unawares;
Kirk-Alloway was drawing nigh,
Where ghaists and houlets nightly cry.

By this time he was cross the ford,
Where in the snaw the chapman smoor'd;
And past the birks and meikle stane,
Where drunken Charlie brak's neck-bane;
And thro' the whins, and by the cairn,
Where hunters fand the murder'd bairn;
And near the tree, aboon the well,
Where Mungo's mither hang'd hersel:
Before him, Doon pours all his floods;
The doubling storm roars thro' the woods;
The lightnings flash from pole to pole!
Near, and more near, the thunders roll;
When, glimmering thro' groaning trees,
Kirk-Aloway seem'd in a bleeze;
Thro' ilka bore the beams were glancing,
And loud resounded mirth and dancing.

Inspiring, bold John Barleycorn!
What dangers thou canst make us scorn:
Wi' tippeny, we fear nae evil;
Wi' usquebae, we'll face the devil!
The swats sae ream'd in Tammie's noddle,
Fair-play, he car'd na deils a boddle:
But Maggy stood, right fair astonish'd,
Till by the heel and hand admonish'd,
She ventur'd forward on the light,
And, wow! Tam saw an unco sight!

Warlocks and witches in a dance,
Nae cotillon brent new frae France,
But hornpipes, jigs, strathspeys and reels,
Put life and mettle in their heels.—
A winnock-bunker in the East,
There sat auld Nick in shape o' beast;
A towzie tyke, black, grim, and large;
To gie them music was his charge:
He screw'd the pipes and gart them skirl,
Till roof and rafters a' did dirl.—
Coffins stood round, like open presses,
That shaw'd the dead in their last dresses;
And (by some deevilish cantraip slight)
Each in its cauld hand held a light;
By which heroic Tam was able
To note upon the haly table,
A murderer's banes, in gibbet-airns;
Twa-span-lang, wee, unchristen'd bairns;
A thief, new cutted frae a rape,
Wi' his last gasp his gab did gape;
Five tomahawks, wi' blood red-rusted;
Five scymitars, wi' murder crusted;
A garter which a babe had strangled;
A knife a father's throat had mangled,
Whom his ain son of life bereft,
The grey hairs yet stak to the heft:
Wi' mair of horrible and awefu',
That even to name wad be unlawfu';
Three lawyers' tongues, turn'd inside out,
Wi' lies seem'd like a beggar's clout;
Three priest's hearts, rotten, black as muck,
Lay stinking, vile, in every neuk.

attempted, some time ago, to take away the bell; but were repulsed by the Alloites, *vi & armis.*

As Tammie glowr'd, amaz'd and curious,
The mirth and fun grew fast and furious;
The piper loud and louder blew;
The dancers quick and quicker flew;
They reel'd, they set, they cross'd, they cleekit,
'Till ilka Carlin swat and reekit,
And coost her duddies on the wark,
And linket at it in her sark.—

Now Tam! O Tam! had thae been queans,
A' plump and strappin in their teens!
Their sarks, instead o' creeshie flainen,
Been snaw-white, seventeen-hunder linen;
Thir breeks o' mine, my only pair,
That ance were plush o' gude blue hair,
I wad hae gien them off my hurdies
For ae blink o' the bonie burdies!
But withered beldams, auld and droll,
Rigwoodie hags wad spean a foal,
Loupin and flingin on a crumock,
I wonder did na turn thy stomach.—

But Tam kend what was what fu' brawlie;
There was ae winsome wench and walie,
That night enlisted in the core,
(Lang after kend on Carrick shore;
For mony a beast to dead she shot,
And perish'd mony a bonnie boat,
And shook baith meikle corn and bear
And kept the country-side in fear)—
Her cutty-sark o' Paisley harn,
That while a lassie she had worn,
In longitude tho' sorely scanty,
It was her best, and she was vauntie.—
Ah! little thought thy reverend graunie,
That sark she coft for her wee Nannie
Wi' twa pund Scots ('twas a' her riches)
Should ever grac'd a dance o' witches!

But here my Muse her wing maun cour,
Sic flights are far beyond her power;
To sing how Nannie lap and flang,
(A souple jad she was and strang,)
And how Tam stood like ane bewitch'd,
And thought his very een enrich'd;

Even Satan glowr'd, and fidg'd fu' fain,
And hotch'd, and blew wi' might and main;
Till first ae caper—syne anither—
Tam lost his reason a' thegither,
And roars out—" Weel done, cutty-sark!"
And in an instant all was dark;
And scarcely had he Maggie rallied,
When out the hellish legion sallied.

As bees bizz out wi' angry fyke,
When plundering herds assail their byke;
As open pussie's mortal foes,
When, pop, she starts before their nose;
As eager rins the market-croud,
When " catch the thief!" resounds aloud;
So Maggy rins, the witches follow,
Wi' mony an eldrich shout and hollo.—

Ah Tam! ah Tam! thou'll get thy fairin!
In hell they'll roast thee like a herrin!
In vain thy Kate awaits thy comin,
Kate soon will be a woesu' woman!!!
Now, do thy speedy utmost, Meg!
And win the key-stane o' the brig;
There at them thou thy tail may toss,
A running stream they dare na cross!
But ere the key-stane she could make,
The fient a tail she had to shake;
For Nannie, far before the rest,
Hard upon noble Maggy prest,
And flew at Tam with furious ettle,
But little kend she Maggy's mettle!
Ae spring brought off her master hale,
But left behind her ain gray tail:
The carlin claught her by the rump,
And left poor Maggy scarce a stump.

Now wha this Tale o' truth shall read,
Ilk man and mother's son, take heed:
Whene'er to drink you are inclin'd,
Or cutty-sarks rin in your mind,
Think, ye may buy the joys o'er dear;
Remember TAM O' SHANTER'S MEARE!

CROSRAGUEL ABBEY.

CROSRAGUEL, Croceregal, or Crofragmol abbey stands in Carrick, one of the subdivisions of the Shire of Ayr, and in the parish of Kirkofwald, two miles from Maybole.

THIS was a Cluniac abbey founded by Duncan, son of Gilbert, Earl of Carrick, in the year 1244, as we are informed by the Chartulary of Paisley. There is a charter of King Robert Bruce to this place, which he therein calls Croceragmer de terra de Dungrelach, given at Berwick the eighteenth year of his reign, and also confirmation of all the churches and lands granted to it by Duncan Neil [Nigellus] Robert, his father, and Edward Bruce, his brother, Earls of Carrick, dated at Cambus-kenneth, the 20th of June, and the twenty-first year of his reign.

THE last abbot of this place was Quintin Kennedy, brother to the Earl of Caffils. The famous George Buchannan had afterwards a considerable sum of money paid him yearly from this abbey, which gave him occasion to denominate himself Pensionarius de Crofragmol. Both the temporalities and spiritualities of this abbey, were by King James VI. annexed to the Bishoprick of Dumblane.

ACCORDING to Keith's Appendix to the History of the affairs of Church and State of Scotland, the revenues of this house were, money 466l. 13s. 4d. Bear 18 c. 7 b. 3 fi. 3½ p. Meal 37 c. Oats 4 c. 15 b. 3 fi. 2½ p.

FOR the following description of this venerable ruin I am indebted to a gentleman resident near the spot, whose name I am not at liberty to mention:

"THE abbey of Corfegal, or Corroguel, stands about half way between the Manse of Kirkofwald and the town of Maybole, near two miles from each; the publick road from Ayr to Port Patrick runs along the North side of the precincts; these contain about eight acres of ground, and were enclosed, at least to the West, the North, and the East, with a stone wall of considerable strength. In this wall there were two gates, one to the North, which seems to have been the principal,

AYRSHIRE.

cipal, another to the South Weſt. Theſe gates were almoſt entire about thirty years ago, but are now, as well as the wall, levelled with the ground; veſtiges, however, both of the gates and the wall, are ſtill viſible, excepting to the South of the abbey; on that ſide there are no remains of any building whatſoever. A wall was perhaps unneceſſary there, as the precincts are bounded by a marſh. The figure of the precincts is too irregular to be comprehended from a bare deſcription: by cutting off a ſmall corner or two they may be reduced to a rhomboid, which is the figure they moſt reſemble.

In the center ſtands the abbey; the ſituation ſeems not extremely happy; it is very low; the ſurface of the ground near it very irregular, ſwelling on all hands into hills. The view from it is of conſequence exceedingly confined towards the Eaſt, however, there is a ſmall interruption in the hills, which opens a proſpect ſomewhat extenſive and pleaſant.

In point of excellent water no place can be better ſupplied, a ſmall ſtream riſing out of a marſh adjoining to the Weſt of the precincts, runs immediately along the South of the abbey; this ſtream, it is thought, was conveyed under the very buildings. The walls of theſe are for the moſt part entire, and have a very venerable and magnificent appearance. A maſterly pen might make them retain ſomething of this even in deſcription, but I am quite unacquainted with buildings of this kind, and know not even their names. The following ſketch of the noble remains of this abbey muſt therefore be extremely imperfect and inelegant; I ſhall notwithſtanding endeavour to make it as intelligible and accurate as I can.

Entering the precincts from the North, where the principal gate ſtood, you have in front what I ſhall call the Cathedral of the Abbey, which ſtands due Eaſt and Weſt; the walls are almoſt entire, about one hundred and ſixty-four feet long, and twenty-two feet high; the architecture in the ſame Gothic taſte which is common in ſtructures of the ſame period; the ſtones in general not very large. There is but one door in all this North ſide and front of the cathedral, which is near the Weſt end of it, conſiderably ornamented, of a conic ſhape, nine feet high, and at the bottom five feet broad. The ground along the

the whole of the building, for about twenty paces from the wall, is enclosed with a bad stone dyke, and set apart for a burying place: but is now seldom used.

Leaving the above-mentioned door you turn to the West end of the cathedral, and go about thirty paces South West, which brings you to what is called the Abbot's New House. It is an oblong tower about thirty feet high; below it there is a large arch, through which you pass before you get to the door of the house, which is immediately on the South East side of the arch; this door leads you up a winding narrow stair, built to the tower, and consisting of three flights of steps; the first flight brings you to a room thirteen feet by eleven, lighted by two windows, three feet high, and two feet and a half broad, the one looking to the South, the other to the North; the second flight brings you to another room exactly of the same dimensions and lighted in the same manner: the third brings you to the top of the tower, which is surrounded by a parapet wall. On the top of the stair-case is a small building, higher than the tower, which is said to have been a bell-house. From the West side of this tower, and at right angles with it, there has been a row of buildings, which are now a heap of ruins; at the South end a Dovecoat of a very singular construction is still extant; the shaft of it is circular, and surrounds a well of excellent water; above five feet from the ground it begins to swell, and continues for six or seven feet, then contracts as it rises, till it comes to a point at the top; in shape therefore it resembles a pear, hanging from the tree, or rather an egg standing on the thickest end; you enter it by a small door on the North, about five feet from the ground; the floor is of stone, and serves also as a covering to the well beneath; the sides within are full of square holes for pigeons; it is lighted from the top by a small circular opening, and is still perfectly entire, sixteen feet perpendicular, and where widest eight feet in diameter.

Returning to the door of the Abbot's House, you go about ten paces due East, along the inside of an high wall, which joins to the other buildings of the abbey; here has been a gate, now in ruins; entering by the place where the gate stood, you find yourself on the South West corner of a court, fifty-two feet square; round this court

there

AYRSHIRE.

there has been a covered way; veftiges of the arches by which the covering was fupported are ftill vifible: in the midft of the court was a well, which is now filled up with rubbifh; walking along the Weft fide of the court you find nothing but a ftrong wall, till you come to the North Weft corner, where is a fmall arched door, the fides of which are much broken down; this door leads into a kind of gallery, eighteen feet broad, and feventy-two feet long; lighted only by three narrow flips to the Weft.

TURNING from this door you walk feventy-two feet along the South wall of the cathedral, which forms the North fide of the court; in this you find three doors, one almoft at the North Weft corner of the court, and two near the North Eaft. Thefe doors are nearly of the fame dimenfions, nine feet high, five feet broad at the bottom, and femicircular at the top. The door at the North Weft corner of the court is almoft oppofite the door in the front or North wall of the cathedral, which we have already mentioned, and leads into the choir. This forms the Weft part of the cathedral, is of an oblong figure, eighty-eight feet long, and twenty-five broad within the walls, lighted by five windows, with pointed arches, ten feet high, and three feet broad at the bottom; there is but one fmall window to the South, at the head of the wall, which has received the light over the covering of the court; on the North wall and near the North Eaft corner of the choir, is a niche in the wall, femicircular at the top, eight feet broad, and four feet high, where it is probable the image of the patron Saint formerly ftood.

THE partition which divides the choir from the church, or Eaft part of the cathedral, is pretty entire, and has been furnifhed with a pair of bells; precifely in the middle of the partition is a door, with a pointed arch, nine feet high, and five feet broad at the bottom, which leads into the church; this ftill retains fomething of its ancient magnificence, is of the fame breadth with the choir, but only feventy-fix feet long; the Eaft end of it is femicircular, or rather triagonal, adorned with three large windows, with pointed arches, eleven feet high and feven feet broad at the bottom; there are fix other windows to the North, and one to the South, of the fame fhape and height, but only fix feet broad.

L   Immediately

Immediately below the South window, and near the South Eaſt corner of the church, ſtands the altar, which has been greatly ornamented, but is now defaced; no veſtiges of any inſcription remain here, or in any part of the abbey. The altar is ſeven feet broad, and four feet high, ſquare, but fretted at the top a little to the left from it; below the moſt Southerly of the largeſt windows, there is a niche in the wall four feet high and two broad, concave at the top, but almoſt without ornament; in the bottom are two hollows made in the ſtone, like the bottom of a plate; this is ſuppoſed to have been a private altar, perhaps that of the family of Caſſilis.

A little to the right of the principal altar is a ſmall door leading to a ruinous ſtair which we ſhall have occaſion to mention immediately. Still farther to the right of the altar, on the ſame wall, is a larger door, ſeven feet high and ſix broad, with a pointed arch, which leads into a high arched room, with a pillar in the middle, and a ſtone bench round the ſides, twenty feet long and fifteen broad, ſaid to be the place where the Confiſtorial Court was held; it is lighted only by one window from the Eaſt; on the left hand, as you enter the room from the church, there is a door which opens on the ruinous ſtair already mentioned. This ſtair has led into a room immediately above the confiſtory, preciſely of the ſame length and breadth, but now level with the floor. From this room you deſcend a few ſteps into the Abbot's Hall, which is twenty feet ſquare, lighted by two ſmall windows to the Eaſt, and one to the Weſt looking in the court.

Returning from the Abbot's Hall into the church, by the ſame door, we find the door in the South Weſt corner of the church, the dimenſions of which have been already given; going out at this door we find ourſelves in the North Eaſt corner of the court; walking five paces from this we come to a door, ſemicircular at the top, eight feet high and five broad which, opens into a room arched in the roof, immediately below the Abbot's Hall, of the ſame breadth and length, and lighted from the Eaſt by two ſmall windows; proceeding from this room to the South Eaſt corner of the court, you find a ruinous arch, about twenty-four feet long, ten feet high, and nine broad, with a ſtone bench on both ſides; this ſeems to have led to a number of cells,

cells, which are now a heap of ruins. Turning from this arch you walk along the South fide of the court, where there is nothing obfervable but feveral fmall doors, leading into ruinous cells; what number of thefe there may altogether have been, it is now impoffible to determine, as the greateft part of them are buried under the rubbifh of their own walls.

The Abbot's Old Houfe, as it is called, is the only building of the abbey we have not hitherto mentioned : this ftands immediately to the South Eaft of the ruinous cells above defcribed. It has been an oblong tower; but the Eaft fide, in which the ftair has been built, is now fallen down, which prevents its dimenfions from being accurately taken; they feem, however, to have been nearly the fame with the dimenfions of the Abbots New Houfe.

The precincts, containing, as above, about eight acres of ground, is at prefent poffeffed by Sir Adam Ferguefon, as it was by his father, upon a tack or leafe from the Chapel Royal, for nineteen years, at a fmall rent, and graffum at entry. Sir Adam fubjects thefe precincts to his tenant, who rents a farm clofe to the abbey; this farm is part of the barony of Balterfan, of which the Manfion Houfe, a fine old building, is ftill remaining, though in ruins, about a quarter of a mile from the Abbey: Sir Adam is the proprietor. The fteading of farm houfes is at prefent near the middle of the precincts.

This view, which fhews the South fide of the ruin, with the remarkable Dovecoat herein defcribed, was drawn A. D. 1789. At a diftance in the back ground appears the Old Houfe of Balterfan.

CROSRAGUEL ABBEY. Plate II.

This view gives the Eaft fide of the Abbey, with the Eaft end of the church and building here called the Confiftorial Court.

CROSRAGUEL ABBEY. Plate III.

This view fhews the North fide of the Abbey, and the Abbot's New Houfe, as feen from the high road leading to Maybole.

They were all drawn A. D. 1789.

TURNBURY CASTLE.

THE next upon the coast are to be seen the old ruins of the ancient castle of Turnberry, upon the North West point of that rocky angle that turns about towards Gervan, and is perhaps the place called by Ptolomee, Perigonium, of a Greek origination, importing round the corner, and suiting the English designation of Turnbury; and that it cannot be Bargeny, as some imagine, the very situation of that castle and recentness of it will abundantly shewe; and to confirme this our conjecture, the Perigonium is Turnberry, from turning of the corner, a tradition among the people there, will not a little induce, viz. that near to this very castle, there was of old a towne of the same name, of which there is no vestige at present to be seen, but that they perceive some remainders of a causeway, and that the reason for this may be, the neighbourhood of the port of the greatest resort in all that coast, at which the first possessors have landed from Ireland, and so might have fixed their habitations near to it, though now the place be but a tract of barren sand.—Thus far Mr. Abbercrombie.

THIS castle belonged to Alexander, Earl of Carrick, who died in the Holy Land, and left an only daughter and heiress named Martha; she, about the year 1274, taking the diversion of hunting, with her women and attendants, met by accident Robert Bruce, Lord of Annandale in Scotland, and Cleveland in England, a very handsome young man, who after the usual salutes and kisses, which Fordun says were customary in courts, would have proceeded on his way; but the Countess being enamoured with him, seized his horses reins, and with a kind of violence, apparently against his will, led him to her castle of Turnbury, where after detaining him above a fortnight, she married him privately, unknown to the king, or to any of the friends of either party, whence it was currently reported that she had obtained her husband by a rape. On this the king, to punish her for her feudal delinquency, in marrying without his consent, seized her castle and estates; but by the interposition of friends, and the payment of a sum of money, Robert Bruce shortly after obtained a full restitution.

AYRSHIRE. 41

This castle was in the hands of the English in the expedition of King Edward I.

A. D. 1306 Bruce having taken shelter in the Isle of Arran, sent a trusty person into Carrick, to learn how his vassals stood affected to his cause, with instructions, that if he found them disposed to assist him, he should make a signal at a time appointed, by lighting a fire on an eminence near the castle of Turnbury. The messenger found the English in the possession of Carrick, the people dispirited, and none ready to take arms; he therefore did not make the signal; but a fire being made about noon on the appointed spot (possibly by accident) both Bruce and the messenger saw it; the former with his associates put to sea, to join his supposed party; the latter to prevent his coming; they met before Bruce reached the shore, when the messenger acquainted Bruce with the unpromising state of his affairs, and advised him to go back; but he obeying the dictates of despair and valor, resolved to persevere and attacking the English, carelessly cantoned in the neighbourhood of Turnbury, put a number of them to the sword, and pillaged their quarters. Percy from the castle heard the uproar, yet did not sally forth against them, not knowing their strength. Bruce with his followers, not exceeding three hundred in number, remained for some days near Turnbury; but succours having arrived from the neighbouring garrisons, he was obliged to seek safety in the mountainous parts of Carrick.

At present, as may be seen in the drawing, little more than the foundations of the building are remaining. There are some vaults beneath it, possibly once sally ports communicating with the water. From this shore is seen the rock of Ailsa, and to the right that of Lamlash, with the craggy mountains of Arran.

This view was drawn A. D. 1789.

COLAINE OR CULZEEN CASTLE.

This castle stands on the coast of Carrick, in a bay to which it gives name; it is elevated on a rock eighty feet above the level of the sea, which it seems to overhang.

HERE formerly stood an ancient fortalice, of which this is in some degree a part. It was the residence of that branch of the family of the Kennedy's, which afterwards succeeded to the title of Caffilis, in the person of Thomas Kennedy, in default of issue male of the elder branch.

AT the bottom of the rock, under the castle, are three caves, one beyond the other, well known for the legendary tales related of them, on which account they are celebrated by Mr. Burns, the Ayrshire Poet, in his excellent poem on Hallow E'en.

IN the account of Carrick, among Mr. M'Farlan's papers, before quoted, the seat itself is called the Cave.

THE Cave (says Mr. Abbercrombie) the mansion house of Sir Archibald Kennedy, of Colaine, takes his name hence: under the outer area of this house there be three natural caves, which enter large at the water mark, from thence they enter upward to a higher, by an easy ascent; but the entry to the third is more difficult, being both low in the entry and strait. In the highest of them there is a spring of good water.

THE edifice here represented was erected by the present Earl, after a plan drawn by Mr. Adams in 1789. When this view was taken it was not quite completed.

THIS castle is admitted here rather on account of the beauty of its situation, than for any pretence it has to antiquity, unless it may be considered as an ancient building repaired.

MACHLIN CASTLE.

THIS castle stands in the town of Machlin; it formerly belonged to the Earls of Loudoun, and gave the second title to that noble family. In 1789, when this drawing was made, it was the property, by purchase, of Gavin Hamilton, Esq.

AYRSHIRE. 45

traced out. In the year 1560 Alexander, Earl of Glencairne, in confequence of an order from the ftates of Scotland, in a great meafure demolifhed this ftately and beautiful pile. A few years afterwards part of the abbey church was repaired, and converted into the parifh church, and as fuch it was ufed till about the year 1775, when being found ruinous and unfafe, it was wholly taken down, and on its fite a very elegant modern church was erected; the fteeple or tower was again repaired A. D. 1789, at the expence of the Earl of Eglington.

A. D. 1513 William Bunfh, abbot of Kilwinning, was flain at the battle of Flodden.

THE laft commendatory abbot of Kilwinning was Gavin Hamilton, of the family of Roplock, a great enemy to John Knox and the congregation, and a fteady friend to the Queen Regent and her daughter, Queen Mary, by whom he was employed in feveral negotiations. He exchanged his abbacy for the Deanry of Glafgow, with Dr. Henry St. Clair, afterwards Bifhop of Rofs, and Prefident of the College of Juftice, which office he held to his death, in the year 1565. Gavin Hamilton was killed at the Water Gate, in the Cannongate, Edinburgh, June 28th, 1571. He had in the year 1552 made Hugh, Earl of Eglington, Jufticiary Chamberlain and Baillie of Kilwinning, and affigned him a confiderable falary for difcharging thofe offices; his grant was conferred by the Queen, and may be feen in the 21ft book of our Public Records, Chart. 77.

At the general diffolution of religious houfes, Alexander, Earl of Glencairn, obtained a grant of this abbey, upon the refignation of Mr. William Melville, of the family of Raeth. In the year 1603 Hugh, Earl of Eglington, got a new grant of the fame, with all the lands and tithes, which had at any time belonged to it, either in property or fuperiority, and they were erected into a temporal lordfhip to him and his heirs; he alfo obtained the patronage of the churches of Kilwinning, Irwin, Dumbarton, Kilmarnock, Ardroffan, and Kilburney: fince which, it appears in Douglas's account of the family of Balfour, of Burleigh, a charter was procured under the great feal, by Michael Balfour, Lord of Balfour and Burleigh, of the lands of the Barony of Kilwinning, to him and his affigns; this was dated the 7th of September,

tember, 1614; but it was not long held by that lord, since Douglas, from the Public Records, cites a charter of confirmation, dated 1615, of the lands of that lordship, formerly resigned to Hugh, the 5th Earl of Eglington. This view was drawn A. D. 1789.

DEAN CASTLE.

THIS was one of the ancient seats of the Boyds, Earls of Kilmarnock, for some time the favourites of King James III. It was forfeited in the year 1745, afterwards sold to the Earl of Glencairne, and in 1789, when this drawing was made, belonged to Miss Scott.

It lies a small distance from the main road leading from Kilmarnock to Stewarton, and consists of a large vaulted square tower, which seems to have been built about the beginning of the fifteenth century; this is surrounded by a court and other buildings, apparently more modern. Upon the tower, under a defaced coat of arms, there is this inscription:

James Lord of
Kilmarnock
Dame Katherine Creyk
Lady Boyd.

THE Lord James, here commemorated, according to Douglas, died 1654. He was a firm adherent to the royal cause, for which he was by Oliver Cromwell excepted from pardon, and fined fifteen hundred pounds sterling.

In this castle, it is said, Lady Margaret (Douglas calls her Mary) sister to King James III. was confined during the life of her husband, Thomas Boyd, Earl of Arran, from whom she was divorced, notwithstanding she had borne him two children. The pretext for this divorce was some legal impediment at the time of marriage. Some say it was a prior contract to the Lord Hamilton.

On her husband and the rest of his family falling under the king's displeasure, she went to Denmark, to acquaint him with it; who

thereupon

AYRSHIRE. 47

thereupon fled for refuge to the courts of France and Flanders. In the mean time King James fent for her. She hoping to make her hufband's peace, obeyed the fummons, when the divorce was procured. After her hufband's death, who died abroad, fhe was married, A. D. 1471, to the Lord Hamilton, then created Earl of Arran.

CORSHILL HOUSE.

This ruin ftands about a mile from Stewarton, in the main road leading from thence to Paifley.

It was the feat of the family of Cunningham. The laft perfon who dwelt in it was Sir David Cunningham, thence denominated of Corfhill. His grandfon is now Lord Lifle. At a fmall diftance from this ruin are fome fmall remains of a more ancient building belonging to the fame family. This view was drawn A. D. 1789.

THE ABBEY OF PAISLEY. RENFREWSHIRE.

The priory of Paifley ftands in the town of that name, in the Shire of Renfrew. It was firft a priory, and afterwards changed into an abbey of Black Monks, brought from Wenlock, in England. It was founded by Walter, fon of Alan, Lord High Steward of Scotland, in the year 1164. It was the common burial place of that noble family, until they became Kings of Scotland; and altho' King Robert II. the firft of this race who attained to that dignity, was buried at Scone, yet neverthelefs his firft Lady, Elizabeth Muir (who has made a great noife in the Scottifh Hiftory) and Euphemia Rofs, his Queen, were both buried here, as likewife Margery Bruce his mother.

The monks of this place are fuppofed to have written a Chronicle of the Affairs of Scotland, called the Black Book of Paifley, from the colour of its cover. This curious monument of antiquity, cited frequently

quently by Buchannan, belonged to the Prefident Spotefwood, and after his death was carried into England by General Lambert, and is now in the King's library, at St. James's.

GEORGE SHAW, abbot of this place, in the year 1484, enlarged and beautified this monaftery; he built the refectory, and other offices neceffary for the monks, the church and the precinct of the convent, and enlarged the gardens and orchards, which he enclofed with a wall of hewn ftone, meafuring about a mile in circuit. In one of the corners of this wall, towards the outer fide, there was a niche, with a ftatue of the Virgin Mary, with this diftich engraven under her feet;

> Hac ne vade via; nifi dixeris Ave Maria:
> Sit femper fine væ; qui tibi dicit Ave;

One of his fucceffors was John Hamilton, natural fon to James, Earl of Arran, who was then Bifhop of Dunkeld, and afterwards Archbifhop of St. Andrews. The Bifhop refigned it in the year 1553, 6to Id. Decembris, with the Queen's confent (refervatis fibi fructibus) in favour of Lord Claud Hamilton, a child of ten years of age, notwithftanding that it is expreffed in the Bulls of Pope Julius, that he was fourteen years old. This Lord Claud was third fon of James, Duke of Chatelherault, Governor of Scotland. He adhered to Queen Mary's intereft, and was at the field of Langfide in the year 1568, for which he was forfeited: and Paifley, thus in the hands of the crown, was beftowed by the Regent upon Robert, fon to William Lord Semple, heritable Baillie of Paifley, and Jufticiary of that regality; but Lord Claud being afterwards reftored to his fortune, was, in the year 1591, by the favour of King James VI. created Lord Paifley. His fon, James, Earl of Abercorn, A. D. 1592, difpofed the abbacy of Paifley in favour of the Earl of Angus, by whom it was alienated, in the year 1653, to William, firft Earl of Dundonald; in his pofterity it continued till the year 1764, when the prefent Earl of Abercorn repurchafed this paternal inheritance of his family. The abbey church appears to have been, when entire, a very grand building: it was in the

the form of a crofs. The great North window is a fine ruin, the arch very lofty, and the middle pillar wonderfully light, and ftill entire; only the chancel now remains, which is divided into a middle and two fide ifles, by lofty columns, whofe capitals are ornamented with grotefque figures, and fupporting Gothic or pointed arches. Here are two ranges of pointed windows, the upper ones remarkably clofe to each other. Both the Weft and North doors are highly decorated with fculpture; indeed the whole outfide has been profufely ornamented. In 1789 this building was fitting up for parochial fervice, with pews and galleries, and when finifhed will be much the handfomeft church in Scotland. Towards the Weft end there are feveral other ruins.

The Earl of Abercorn's burial place here, is faid to be famous for a remarkable echo; not having heard of it I did not vifit it. It is thus defcribed by Mr. Pennant. " The Earl of Abercorn's burial place is by much the greateft curiofity in Paifley; it is an old Gothic chapel, without pulpit or pew, or any ornament whatever; but it has the fineft echo perhaps in the world, when the end door, the only one it has, is fhut; the noife is equal to a loud, and not very diftant clap of thunder: if you ftrike a fingle note of mufic you hear the found gradually afcending, till it dies away, as if at an immenfe diftance, and all the while diffufing itfelf through the circumambient air. If a good voice fings, or a mufical inftrument is well played upon, the effect is inexpreffibly agreeable."—In this chapel is the monument of Margery Bruce; fhe lies recumbent, with her hands clofed in the attitude of prayer: over her was once a rich arch, with fculptures of her arms.

Mr. Pennant likewife, in his defcription of this place, fpeaking of the garden wall beforementioned, fays, " The garden wall, a very noble and extenfive one, of cut ftone, conveys fome idea of the ancient grandeur of this place; by a rude infcription, ftill extant, on the North Weft corner, it appears to have been built by George Shaw, the Abbot. in the year 1484; the fame gentleman who four years after procured a charter for the town of Paifley: the infcription is too fingular to be omitted.

> Thy callit the Abbot George of Shaw,
> About my Abby gart make this waw,
> An hundred,* four hundredth zear,
> Eighty four, the date but weir,
> Pray for his falvation
> That laid this noble foundation."

The revenues of this abbey are thus given in Keith's Appendix, Cluniac Abbey of Paifley, in the Shire of Renfrew. Money 2468 l. † Bear 40 c. 12 b.   Meal 72 c. 3 b. 3 f. 1½ p.   Oats 43 c. 1 b. 1 f. 1 p. Cheefe 705 ft.

---

* This is evidently an error, probably a typographical one; it fhould be a thoufand.
† Scots.

TWEEDALE.

THE CROSS CHURCH, PEEBLES.

This is part of the Conventual church, built, according to Boecius Major and others, by King Alexander III. A. D. 1257. Some say it was erected on the spot where the reliques of St. Nicholas, a martyr, were discovered; but from the account of this discovery, preserved at Peebles, it appears that that event did not happen till May, 7th, 1262. Possibly a new church, or some addition to the old one, might have been built on this occasion. Fordun says 1261, and the Chronicle of Melrofs places this discovery in 1260. This St. Nicholas was a Scotch Bishop, of the order of Culdees; he is supposed to have suffered martyrdom during the persecution of Maximian, about the year of our Lord 296.

Fordun thus relates the circumstances of finding these reliques. In the same year, i. e. 1261, 7th Id. May, and the 13th of King Alexander, there was found at Peebles, in the presence of diverse respectable persons, presbyters, clerks, and burgesses, a magnificent and venerable cross, but by whom it had been hidden, or in what year, was totally unknown. It was however believed, that when the persecution by Maximian raged in Britain, about the year of our Lord 296, it had been hidden by some pious persons. Shortly after, in the same place, and about four paces from the spot where the cross had been discovered, was found an urn of stone, containing the ashes and bones of a human body, which seemed to have been dismembered limb by limb. No one could tell whose remains these were. A certain man, however, affirmed them to be the bones of the person whose name was found written on the stone on which the holy cross was

found,

found, for it was written on the outside of the said stone, the place of St. Nicholas, the Bishop. In the place where the cross was found many miracles were, and are still performed by the said cross; so that crouds of people flock thither, devoutly offering their prayers and oblations to God. Wherefore the King, by the advice of the Bishop of Glasgow, caused a handsome church to be erected to the honour of God and the Holy Cross.

This monastery was possessed by Red Friars. King Robert II. grants to Friar Thomas described as Capellana suo, pratum regium juxta villam de Peebles; and Frere Thomas Ministre de Sancta Crucis de Peebles occurs in Prynn's Collections.

The monastery was built in the form of a square. The church, which formed the South side, measured on the outside, one hundred and two feet; its width was thirty-two; the height of its side walls twenty-four feet from the level of the floor; they were three feet thick. The offices of the convent formed the three other sides. From some projecting stones, calculated to receive a roof, it appears, that there were some buildings against the North wall of the church. The cloisters were on the West side; the dwelling houses were only twenty-two feet deep.

The whole was built with whin stone, except the angles, doors, windows, cornices, &c. which were all of a white free-stone, remarkably good and durable; the arches of the doors and windows are pointed.

The church had four doors, two on the South side, one on the North leading from the convent, and one in the West end, all decorated with neat mouldings. There have evidently been four, if not five windows on the front or fore wall, each fifteen feet high from the sole to the top of the arch, and five feet seven inches wide; a more modern one in the East gable sixteen feet high and seven wide. In the fore wall of the church, between the third window from the West and the door on the East of that window, there has plainly been an aperture and arch formed at the first building of the church; it is of a particular construction, four feet wide, and two and a half high, on the outside; but increasing to between six and seven feet in width, and eight feet in height on the inside, with decorations of free stone pro-

jecting

jecting beyond the line of the wall, not done in any other part of the church, which makes it highly probable that the urn, containing the reliques of St. Nicholas, and the Crofs found near them, were depofited there; the head and tranfverfe beam of the Crofs within the church, where the niche, or opening in the wall was made to widen for its reception, and the foot of the Crofs, and of the ftone containing it, projected without the wall on the outfide, or at leaft was vifible there. Thus pious perfons might offer up their prayers, contemplating thefe holy reliques, both within and on the outfide of the church.

This monaftery continued to be ufed as fuch till about the year 1560, when the Reformation took place, and its revenues were difpofed of to different perfons; that part which fell to the crown was afterwards given by King James VI. to Murray, of Black Barony, to whofe defcendants it ftill belongs. Before the fuppreffion the borough of Peebles having been burned by the Englifh, was, for fafety, rebuilt on the other fide of the Eddeftone water, on a fpot nearer this houfe. The church being more convenient for parochial fervice than that of St. Andrew, was after the Diffolution fubftituted for it, and a tower was then built at the Weft end of it.

The convent was fuffered gradually to fall to decay; fome of the vaults and cells were, however, ufed for lodging perfons infected with the plague, in 1666; and in the beginning of this century thirty feet was walled off from the eaft end of the church, for the publick fchool, which was held here, and galleries were erected in the remaining part to compenfate for this diminution.

In this ftate it continued till the year 1784, when the roof, galleries, and feats becoming decayed through age, a new church was built in the town, and the Crofs Church was ftripped of its feats and roof; but the walls, by a commendable act of the magiftrates and council, were ordained to continue as a venerable monument of antiquity.

This view was drawn A. D. 1790.

ST. ANDREW'S CHURCH, PEEBLES.

This was formerly the parifh church. It was dedicated to St. Andrew. The time of its conftruction is not known; but it is faid to have been dedicated by Joceline, Bifhop of Glafgow, who died A. D. 1199. To judge by the ftyle of its architecture it feems of confiderable antiquity, all the arches of its doors and windows being femicircular, or at leaft fome fegment of a circle; from an infpection of its remains it feems to have been full as large as the Crofs Church.

BEFORE the Reformation, the town having been rebuilt, changed its fituation, and being brought nearer to the Crofs Church, that was, after the Diffolution, appropriated to parochial ufes, and St. Andrew's fuffered to fall to ruin, its roof having been demolifhed by Cromwell's foldiers, who ufed it for a ftable.

THE tower, which is fquare, is ftill ftanding with fome fragments of the fide walls of the church. The church-yard, from a number of modern tomb ftones, appears to be ftill ufed as a burial ground.

IN this church were twelve altarages, founded and endowed by the moft ancient families of the neighbouring gentry of the Shire of Tweedale. Here too was annually chofen, on the Monday before Michaelmas, the Deacon of the Corporation of Weavers, of the borough of. Peebles. This view was drawn A. D. 1790.

NID PATH CASTLE.

THIS caftle ftands on a rock, projecting over the North bank of the river Tweed, which here runs through a deep narrow glen, well wooded on both fides, and towards the land on the North fide, commanded an important pafs.

BY whom, or at what period it was built, is not known. It was formerly the feat of the Frafers, Lords of Oliver Caftle, in Tweedie Muir, and from them, about the year 1312, came to the Hays, Lords of Yefter: one of which family was afterwards, by King James III. A. D. 1487, created Lord Hay of Yefter, whofe defcendant, John, the eighth Lord Hay, was on the 1ft of December, 1646, raifed to the dignity of the Earl of Tweedale.

WHEN King Charles II. marched for England, John, fecond Earl of Tweedale, garrifoned his caftle of Nid Path, for his Majefty's fervice, which held out againft Oliver Cromwell longer than any place South of the Forth.

THE

The family of Tweedale being greatly impoverished by their adherence to the Royal cause, sold this, and several other estates, to William, the first Duke of Queensberry, whose son was created Earl of March and Ruthenglen, Lord Nid Path; and this castle was for some time the residence of the Earls of March: it at present belongs to his Grace the Duke of Queensberry.

The walls of this castle are eleven feet thick; a stair-case was lately cut into the thickness of them, without damaging the building. It is now, however, in ruin, part of it having fallen down.

The banks hereabouts, particularly from the high road, a little above the castle, afford a most beautiful prospect, terminated by a view of the town and bridge of Peebles.

Dr. Pennicuik, in his description of Tweedale, informs us, this building was of old called the Castle of Peebles: he thus celebrates it:

> The noble Nid Path Peebles overlooks,
> With its fair bridge and Tweed's meandering brooks;
> Upon a rock it proud and stately stands,
> And to the fields about gives forth commands.

This view was drawn A. D. 1790.

AUCHINCASS CASTLE. EVANDALE.

This castle is situated in Evandale, in the parish of Kirkpatrick, on the West side of the river Evan, near its junction with the water of Garfell, about three miles South West from Moffat; it stands on an eminence, surrounded by a morass.

The building was, when entire, a square, flanked by a round tower on each angle. The walls were remarkably thick and high, the whole surrounded by a deep double ditch. Great part of the building is now fallen, as may be seen by the view.

Anno 1072 this place belonged to Hugh de Graham, and continued in that family for many generations; from him it came to the Johnsons of Colhead, and was very lately the property of a gentleman of the name of Milligan. This view was drawn A. D. 1790.

DRUMMELZIER CASTLE. TWEEDALE.

DRUMMELZIER Caſtle is ſituated cloſe to the river Tweed. It was formerly the ſeat of the powerful family of Tweedie, who had great poſſeſſions in the South of Scotland. A ſmall caſtle, ſituated on the point of a ſteep conical rock, about half a mile from Drummelzier, was uſed by the Lords of Tweedie, as a ſort of reduit or citadel. This fortalice, of which only a few walls are ſtanding, was called the Thanes caſtle, vulgarly Tennis Caſtle. Both this and Drummelzier Caſtle went by marriage to the Hays. A deſcendant of that family is the preſent proprietor.

DUMMELZIER caſtle, in 1790, when this drawing was taken, was much out of repair. Its form and ſituation will be beſt underſtood from the annexed view.

TWEEDMUIR CHURCH.

THE annexed view, which ſhews the church of Tweedmuir, and the adjacent picturefque country, was drawn from the back of the Bild Inn, A. D. 1790.

THE mount on which this church ſtands is generally ſuppoſed to be an ancient tumulus, and is vulgarly called a Roman work.

NOTHING can be more romantic than the hills hereabouts; a group of them here repreſented, when ſeen in a particular point of view, with a particular light upon them, require ſmall aſſiſtance from fancy to make them reſemble a couchant lion, or ſome other large four-footed animal, in a cumbent poſture.

CLACK-

CLACKMANNANSHIRE.

CLACKMANNAN TOWER.

THIS tower is pleasantly situated on the summit of a hill, commanding an extensive and beautiful prospect over the adjacent tract of country. It was long the seat of the chief of the Bruces. The large square tower here represented is called Robert Bruce's tower; his two-handed sword and helmet were not long ago, and probably still are, preserved here. Near the tower stands the little town of Clackmannan.

THE Bruces are said to have had a file or string of castles, of which this and another in Sterlingshire were two; they were all within sight of each other, so that they could communicate by signal.

WHEN Clackmannan first belonged to the Bruces is uncertain. There is a charter quoted by Douglas as early as the time of King David II. dated 9th of December, 1359; wherein that King grants to Sir Robert Bruce (whom he therein styles his dearly beloved relation) the castle and manor of Clackmannan, with diverse other lands, lying within the Sheriffdom of Clackmannan.

LOCH LEVEN CASTLE. KINROSSHIRE.

LOCH LEVEN CASTLE stands in an island measuring about eight English acres, which island is situated nearly in the middle of a loch or lake, about twelve miles in circumference, and in many places twenty-four fathoms deep. It is not known when this castle was built. It occurs in history as early as the year 1335, when it was besieged by Sir John de Sterling.

The following account of that siege is in substance given by Fordun. In the year 1315, in the midst of Lent, Sir John de Sterling, a soldier in the King of England's service, with a great number of Anglefied Scots, among whom were Michael de Arnot, Michael and David de Wemys, and Richard de Melville, Knights, with many others who had embraced the English party, assembled to besiege the castle of Loch Leven, and reconnoitering the borders of the lake, and seeing that the castle would not be easily taken, established their quarters at Kinross, surrounding the church with a fortress; thereby converting the house of God to a den of thieves. Alan de Vipont was then Governor of the castle, and had with him James Lambyn, a citizen of St. Andrews, and many other brave and robust Scotchmen. The siege for a while went on in the ordinary manner; but the besiegers gaining little ground, had recourse to stratagem, and in order to overflow the castle and drown the garrison, constructed a strong and high dam, with turf and hard rammed earth cross the recess of the water of Leven, where it empties itself; at this work the neighbouring people, women as well as men, worked incessantly; they also, by channels cut in the earth, drew down the waters of Leven to the town of Kinross.

The festival of the blessed Margaret, Queen of Scotland, approaching, which was annually celebrated at Dumfermling, Sir John de Sterling thought it necessary for form sake to attend, taking several of his people with him; the remainder he disposed of in the best manner for carrying on the siege; but the blessed Servanus, the protector of the Islanders, inspired them with the following mode of defence.

The governor and garrison informed of Sterling's absence, and being in want of victuals, firing, and all other necessaries, secretly detached four valiant men in a light boat, and provided with proper instruments to destroy the dam; they got out on the East side of the castle, unperceived by the besiegers, and after labouring almost the whole night, despairing of accomplishing their purpose, had determined to desist. But one of them suggesting that they should persist a little longer, and that he would promise them help from the faith he had in St. Servanus, resuming their work, the water began to ooze through the dam by drops,
which

which they obferving, in hafte returned to their boat, and regained the caftle, carring the joyful news to their comrades, who were thereby filled with courage.

The water continued by degrees to widen the breach, and within the fpace of two hours ran out with great impetuofity; it having been more than a month in collecting. And fuch was its fury, that it fwept away not only the tents, fheds, booths, and cottages of the Englifh, and of thofe lodged on the banks of the lake, carrying their horfes and harnefs to the fea, but alfo tore up and carried away the banks themfelves of even great diftricts.

It being now quite day, the garrifon of the caftle, unanimoufly, as had been previoufly fettled, embarked themfelves with warlike inftruments for the fort, which the foldiers there obferving, and being under great aftonifhment, quickly fallied forth to meet them, when many of each party were wounded with arrows; the Englifh at length, though with difficulty, were obliged to fly; on which the Scots joyfully entered the fort, and obtained a confiderable booty, befides provifions, all which they conveyed away with them. The news of this event having been carried to John de Stirling, he bound himfelf by oath not to retire from the caftle till he had completely demolifhed it, and punifhed the garrifon with death. But the providence of God, which is ever watchful over his faithful fervants, depreffed the affairs of the Englifh, and raifed thofe of the Scotch, and in a fhort time delivered them from the Englifh yoke, under which they had been feverely oppreffed. John de Stirling feeing it was not for his intereft to perfevere, and having, as a note fuggefts, made a fort of treaty of peace with the garrifon of the caftle, difgracefully retired home, not without the ftain of perjury.

It is remarkable that Fordun here makes this defence a kind of miracle performed by St. Servanus, as tutelar Saint of the ifle; but this is not the ifland in which St. Servanus's Monaftery formerly ftood, and it does not appear he was protector of any other.

Maitland, who places this event in the year 1334, doubts the truth of the ftory, and offers feveral fubftantial arguments in fupport of his opinion.

It

It is said this castle was anciently a royal residence. It was granted by King Robert III. to Douglas, thence probably stiled Lord of Loch Leven; but what makes this castle the most remarkable is, that it was the prison wherein the unfortunate Queen Mary was confined, and from whence she made her escape. It had occasionally been used as a prison, both before and after that time.

The castle in 1790, when these drawings were made, consisted of a rectangular wall, enclosing a small area, flanked by little towers, some of them round; with some ruined walls, said to be those of the chapel and apartment where Queen Mary was confined. The keep is a square tower; it stands in the North East angle of the area; in it, as I have read (for I could not get in to see it) there is a pit or dungeon, and a vaulted room over it; the chief entrance is through a gate in the North side.

On the outside of the castle, chiefly towards the East, are several ancient trees, particularly the remains of an ash, which appears, when entire, to have been of a great size. This view shews the inside of the castle and the keep, as viewed from the South West.

LOCHOR CASTLE.

This Castle is built on a peninsula on the South side of the Loch of Lochor, in the Shire of Kinross, and was founded by Duncan de Lochor, in the reign of Malcolm IV. King of Scotland, anno 1160. It consisted of a strong square tower, with many lower buildings, surrounded by a wall, with round towers, washed by the waters of the Loch, which abounds with pike and perch.

In the reign of King Alexander II. Adam de Lochor was Sheriff of Perth, David de Lochor is in 1255 also Sheriff. In 1289 Hugo de Lochor is Vicecomes de Fife, as is Constantinus in 1292. David de Lochor is named in Ragman's roll anno 1296. In 1315 Thomas de Lochor is in the Parliament at Ayr, that tailzied the crown, and his seal is appended to that act. In the reign of King Robert I. this estate fell to the son of a gentleman, Adam de Valloniis, who had married a daughter

ter of the Barons of Lochor. It continued in this family for a considerable time, and then came to Sir Andrew Wardlaw, of Torry, who married the eldest daughter of D. Jacobus de Valloniis, in whose family it remained till the time of King Charles I. Over the chief entry to the tower is inscribed Robertus de Wardlaw, who greatly fortified and repaired this castle. After the Wardlaws it came into the possession of Sir John Malcolm, whose descendant, Sir Michael, lately sold what remained of this ancient Barony to ——Park, Esq.

In this Castle Christopher Seaton, who had married the sister of King Robert Bruce, and had assisted at the slaughter of Comyn, at Dumfries, was taken, and by the order of King Edward I. was beheaded at Dumfries, anno 1306.

LINLITHGOWSHIRE.

THE PALACE OF LINLITHGOW.

This Palace is situated on an eminence near the Northern bank of a fine Loch or Lynn, from which, it is said, the town of Linlithgow takes its name.

King Edward I. built a palace on this spot, in which he resided for a whole winter; but in 1307 it was taken and demolished by one Binny, a Scotchman. In the reign of King Edward III. it was again in the hands of the English, as is proved by an order, still extant, granting the custody of the hospital to John Swanland; a copy of this order is printed in Sir Joseph Ayloffe's Calendar of Charters.

A. D. 1424, according to Fordun, this palace was burned, as was also the town and nave of the church, by night; but by whom it was rebuilt is not known, nor is it said whether this fire was occasioned by accident or treachery. It is at present, 1790, a magnificent edifice, of a square form, the greater part of it five stories high; the Kings, James V. and VI. ornamented it greatly. The inside is embellished with good sculpture, considering the time in which it was executed. Over an inner gate are niches, in which were, according to Lesley, in his history of Scotland, the statue of the Pope, who sent the famous consecrated sword and helmet to James V. and that of one of his Cardinals.

On an outward gate, detached from the building, are the four orders of knighthood borne by the King, viz. the Garter, Thistle, Holy Ghost, and Golden Fleece. Within the palace is a handsome square; one side is more modern than the other, having been built by James VI. The building was kept in good repair till the year 1746, when being used as a barrack, it was accidentally fet on fire by the King's troops. The pediments over the windows are dated 1619.

In one of the other fides is a room ninety-five feet long, thirty feet fix inches wide, and thirty-three high; at one end is a gallery with three arches, perhaps intended for a band of mufick: narrow galleries run quite round the old part, to preferve the communication with the apartments. The parliament chamber is a handfome room.

Here was born on the 8th of December, 1542, the unfortunate Queen Mary. Her father, James V. then dying at Falkland of a broken heart, for the mifcarriage at Solway Mofs, foretold the miferies that hung over her and Scotland. " It came," faid he, " with a lafs, and will be loft with one." The chapel was built by James V. The church is a handfome building, and fome of the windows are extremely elegant. Here is ftill fhewn the aifle where James IV.* faw the apparition,

---

* Some time ago was found at Home Caftle the remains of a body, in an Ox hide; it had an iron chain round the loins, and was therefore fuppofed to have been James IV. who was well known to wear an iron chain round his loins, by way of penance, for having been acceffary to his father's death; he moreover conftantly added a link to this chain every year. His being found in Home Caftle is thus accounted for : at the battle of Flodden the Earl of Hume with his troops kept aloof; when it is faid, the King efcaping to him much wounded, threatened to call him to a fevere account, for being one of the caufes of the lofs of the battle. The Earl dreading the King's refentment, is faid to have murthered him, and buried him privately in Hume Caftle.

In contradiction to this account, it was generally fuppofed that the body of that King was brought to the abbey of Sheen, near Richmond, in Surry, and there kept till the Pope's permiffion could be had to bury it, he having died under the fentence of excommunication. The Pope's Bull taking off that fentence is printed in Rymer. The above receives fome corroboration from the following letter written by Queen Catherine to King Henry VIII. which was printed in the London Magazine, to which it was communicated by Arthur Collins, author of the Peerage, &c. This letter was copied from the Manufcript Collection of Gregory King, Lancafter Herald.

QUEEN CATHERINE TO KING HENRY.

SIR,

MY Lord Havard hath fent me a letter open to your grace, within one of mine, by which you will fee at length the great victory that our Lord hath given your fubjects in your abfence; and for this caufe it is no need therein to trouble your grace with long writing; but to my thinking the battle hath been on your grace, and all your realme, the greateft honour that could be, and more than you fhould wyn of the crown of France; thanked be God for it; and I

am

rition, that warned him of the impending fate of the battle of Flodden. The West end of the church seems more modern than the rest, and is said to have been built by a Bishop, as a penance enjoined him by the Pope, for incontinency. On this church is a handsome spire, with a crown on the top. It is now used for parochial service. Lately in digging a grave a basso relievo, neatly cut in stone, was found; the subject was Christ's Passion, of which there were only two parts, the first, Christ's Praying in the Garden, the second, Christ Healing Malchus's Ear; they were both inclosed in Gothick pannels, and measured about two feet in height, and not quite so much in breadth.

am sure your grace forgetteth not to do this, which shall be cause to send you many moe such victories, as I trust he shall doe. My husband, for hastiness, with Rouge Crosse I could not send your grace the piece of the King of Scots coat, which John Glynn now bringeth. In this your grace shall see how I can keep my promise, sending you for banners a King's coat; I thought to send himself to you, but our Englishmen would not suffer it. It should have been better for him to have been in peace, than to have this reward. All that God sendeth is for the best. My Lord of Surrey, my Henry, would fain know your pleasure in burying of the King of Scots body; for he hath written to me so. With the next messenger your grace's pleasure may be therein known; and with this I make an end, praying God to send you home shortly, for without this no joy here can be accomplished, and for the same I pray; and now go to our lady at Walsinghame, that I promised so long ago to see at Voburne the XVI of September——I send your grace herein a bill found in a Scottish man's purse, of such things as the French King sent to the said King of Scots, to make warr against you, beseeching you to send Mathew hither, as soon as the messenger cometh to bring me tidings from your grace.

Your wife and true Servant,
KATHERINE.

The sword and dagger of King James IV. are now preserved in the Heralds Office, where they were lodged by the Earl of Surrey.

Stowe says, that on the Dissolution of the Abbey of Sheene, King James IV's body was thrown into a waste room, amongst old timber, lead, and stone.

STIRLINGSHIRE.

ALMOND HOUSE.

ALMOND HOUSE or CASTLE ſtands on an eminence about half a mile South of the great road leading from Linlithgow to Stirling. It conſiſts of two old towers, with a modern addition at the Eaſt end, ſeemingly of the time of Charles I. or II. though the tenant ſaid the addition was made about fifty or ſixty years ago, but ſeemed to ſpeak only from conjecture. Part of the tower appears very ancient.

THIS houſe, according to Taylor and Skinner's Map of the roads, belonged formerly to the Earls of Errol; but in 1790, when this view was taken, was the property of John Forbes, of Callendar, Eſq.

BRUCE'S CASTLE.

THIS caſtle ſtands on a rocky eminence, about ſix miles South Eaſt from Stirling, and near a mile and a half Eaſt of the main road leading from Falkland to that town.

FROM the traces of walls, &c. it ſeems, when entire, to have occupied a conſiderable area. Some vaults are ſtill remaining. The tenant ſaid, that there was an iron door, which was taken away by Mr. Nicholſon, the preſent proprietor, who converted it into a door to ſome of his ſervants offices. Mr. Nicholſon married the daughter of Sir William Maxwell, of Springkeld.

THIS was one of the file of caſtles mentioned in the deſcription of Clackmannan, and is viſible at a conſiderable diſtance.

THIS view was drawn A. D. 1790.

THE NUNNERY OF EMANUEL, OR MANUEL.

This nunnery is situated on the borders of Stirlingshire, upon the West bank of the water of Avon, about a mile above the bridge of Linlithgow, in the parish of Moranside or Muiravonside. It was founded about the year 1156 by King Malcolm IV. surnamed the Maiden, and was a priory occupied by nuns of the Bernardine or Cistertian order, to whom belonged thirteen convents in Scotland. Besides the endowments bestowed by the royal founder, it received considerable donations from others at different periods. King William, surnamed the Lion, made a grant of the tenth of all his revenues in the shire and borough of Linlithgow, both money and victuals. Alexander II. made a donation of the mills of Linlithgow, with all their sequels and appurtenances; and Roger de Avenel bestowed on the holy sisters a chalder of wheat, to be paid by him and his heirs, out of his barns of Abercorn, at Christmas, yearly.

The prioress of this place, whose name was Christina, swore fealty to Edward I. July 4, 1292, * as did her successor, named Alice, at Linlithgow, in 1296. †

This nunnery had possessions in the shires of Edinburgh and Ayr, as well as in those of Linlithgow and Stirling, as appears by an order of Edward, to the Sheriffs of those shires, to reinstate the prioress in possession of her land, within their several jurisdictions, in consequence of her having sworn fealty to that Monarch.

When the list of ecclesiastical revenues was drawn up in 1562, those of Emanuel amounted to fifty-two pounds, fourteen shillings, and eight-pence Scots, three chalders of bear, seven chalders of meal, with a large quantity of salmon. ‡

Of this nunnery little remains, except the West end of the church. This fragment contains an arched door or gateway, with three small

---

* Rymer's Fœdera, tom. 2. p. 572.
† Keith on Religious Houses.
‡ Keith's Appendix.

Gothic

Gothic windows over it, and over thefe a circular one. This ftructure is of hewn ftone, but unadorned; yet there is an elegant fimplicity in it, and, with the beauty of the furrounding objects, it makes a very picturefque appearance. Part of the South wall of the church was ftanding till the beginning of the year 1788, when the river having rifen to an unufual height, it was fwept away by the violence of the waters, with part of the bank, ufed as a cemetery. William Forbes, Efq. of Callendar, the proprietor, caufed the bank of the river to be repaired, which will probably protect thefe remains from farther injury.

This monaftery came into the hands of the crown by the forfeiture of the Earl of Callendar and Linlithgow, to whofe predeceffor it had been given fome time after the Reformation. Near this nunnery, but on the oppofite fide of the river, lies the field where the battle was fought between the Earls of Lenox and Angus, during the minority of James V. in which the former was defeated and flain. Sir Robert Sibbald, in his Hiftory of Stirlingfhire, fays, near to Emanuel fome curious capellaries are found.—Emanuel is a Hebrew word, fignifying God with us. It is faid the tomb of the priorefs, Alice, was to be feen here a few years ago, upon which was her figure, with a diftaff; an uncommon inftrument to be put in the hands of a priorefs.

This was drawn A. D. 1789.

STIRLING CASTLE.

This caftle is undoubtedly of great antiquity. When it was firft built is unknown. The natural ftrength of the rock on which it ftands, efpecially before the ufe of artillery and bombs, muft have always caufed it to be occupied and fortified. Old chronicles fay, it was fortified by Agricola, and alfo by the Picts. It was called by the Monkifh writers, Mons Dolorum. Its name of Stryveling is faid to have originated from its being the hill of ftrife.

About the middle of the Ninth century, the Scots, under Kenneth II. having expelled the Picts, and being defirous of obliterating every memorial of them, deftroyed this caftle, but Donald V. being taken prisoner by the Northumbrians, obtained his liberty by paying a large sum of money, as a ransom, and yielding up all his dominions on the South side of the Forth to the Northumbrians, and those on the South side of the Clyde, with the town of Dumbarton, to the Cumbrians. The Northumbrians taking possession of the territory ceded to them, rebuilt the castle of Stirling and strongly garrisoned it. It continued about twenty years in the possession of the Northumbrian Saxons; but was afterwards, with the lands South of Forth, restored to the Scots, on condition they should assist the Northumbrians against the Danes.

STIRLING CASTLE was, in the tenth century, the rendezvous for the troops of Kenneth III. when invaded by the Danes, whence he marched to the battle of Longarty. In the twelfth century this castle is spoken of in history, as a place of great importance. In 1174, William the Lion having made an unsuccefsful expedition into England, was taken prisoner, and detained twelve months, after which he stipulated for his ransom, to pay a large sum of money by a certain day; and as a security for the payment, delivered into the hands of the English, the four principal fortreſses of his kingdom, Stirling, Edinburgh, Roxburgh, and Berwick: part of the money being unpaid, was remitted by King Richard I. and the castles restored on condition that William should contribute a sum of money to the crusade.

STIRLING CASTLE was occasionally the residence of the Scottish kings, but not a fixed palace, till the family of Stewart mounted the throne. It was the place of nativity of James II. who often resided at it after he came to the crown; and here he perpetrated the murder of William Earl of Douglas, whom he stabbed with his own hand.

THE royal apartments were then in the North West corner of the castle, and are at present the residence of the Fort Major, and partly occupied by the armory: the closet where the murder was committed, still goes by the name of Douglas's room.

JAMES III. took particular pleasure in this castle, and erected several new buildings in it. He built a large hall now called the Parliament-house, in which several parliaments have been held; he also erected the Chapel Royal, which he largely endowed, and procured to be made collegiate;

collegiate; this chapel was pulled down by James VI. who on its fite erected the prefent chapel. James V. was crowned here, and here refided during his minority, and received his education; he built the prefent palace, which is a fquare all of hewn ftone, adorned with fculpture; in the centre is a fmall fquare court, called the Lion's Den, from the King's lions having been kept there. The palace contains many large and elegant apartments; the ground ftory has been converted into a barrack for the private foldiers; the upper ftory gives a houfe for the governor, and lodgings for the officers.

OPPOSITE to the palace is a chapel of hewn ftone, built by James VI. for the baptifm of Prince Henry, in 1594; it is now employed as a ftore room; and here is preferved the hulk of a boat, in which that King caufed the provifions to be drawn at this ceremony; and in the roof hangs a piece of fquare wood, in which are carved models of the caftles of Edinburgh, Stirling, Dumbarton, and Blacknefs.

A STRONG battery, called the French Battery, points to the bridge; it was probably fo called from being conftructed by engineers of that nation. Great additions were made to the works here, by order of Queen Ann, fome of them never completed.

ADJOINING to the North fide of the caftle is an eminence containing a few acres, which being fortified, makes a part of the caftle; it is called the Nether Bailey. Here is the well which fupplies the garrifon.

ON the South Weft fide of the caftle is the park, enclofed by a ftone wall; this, with feveral other pieces of ground round the garrifon, form a jurifdiction, called the Conftabulary of the caftle. At the Eaft end of the park was a royal garden; veftiges of the walks and parterres are ftill vifible. In the garden is a mount of earth in form of a table, called the Knot, where, according to tradition, the court fometimes held Fêtes Champetres. Poffibly this might be the round table mentioned by Barbour, if fo, it was here King James IV. ufed to amufe himfelf with the paftime, called the Knights of the Round Table, of which he is faid to have been peculiarly fond.

THE

STIRLINGSHIRE.

THE lordſhip and caſtle of Stirling was the uſual dowry of the Queen of Scotland, at leaſt after the acceſſion of the Stewarts.

ON the North Weſt of the caſtle is a ſteep path leading to the town; this is called Ballochgeick. James V. who uſed often to travel through the country in diſguiſe, for different purpoſes, when queſtioned who he was, always anſwered, the Good Man of Ballochgeick.

THIS caſtle has been the ſcene of many warlike feats, having been repeatedly beſieged, taken, diſmantled, and rebuilt by different parties, during the wars between the Engliſh and Scots, as well as in their civil diſſenſions.

A. D. 1297, it being in the hands of the Engliſh, was abandoned by Sir Marmaduke de Twenge, and ſeized by Wallace, for the Scots, who held it a year, and then deſtroyed and abandoned it; it was, however, in a few weeks re-occupied and repaired by King Edward. It was again taken by the Scots in 1299.

A. D. 1303 it capitulated to Sir John de Foulis, for want of proviſion; and was the next year, i. e. 1304, retaken by King Edward, after a long defence, in which the garriſon was reduced to twenty-eight men: in this ſiege Edward is ſaid to have battered it with engines, that threw ſtones of two hundred pounds weight; and Fordun ſays, that he cauſed all the lead to be taken off the monaſtery of St. Andrew's, and carried to Stirling, for the conſtruction of his machines.

A. D. 1333 it yielded to the Baliol party, and, as ſome ſay, was diſmantled by directions from the Engliſh Court; but in 1336 was rebuilt by the orders of King Edward III. ſtrongly garriſoned, and the command of it given to Sir Thomas Ruckby.

A. D. 1337 it was beſieged by the Scots under Sir William Douglas, of Liddeſdale, and Sir Andrew Murray, who lay two months before it, but was relieved by King Edward in perſon. Next year the ſiege was renewed, and again raiſed by the Engliſh Monarch; but in 1339 the Scots, under Douglas and Murray, took it: after which the Engliſh were never able to penetrate ſo far into Scotland.

THE laſt reduction of this fortreſs by a ſiege, was in 1651, when Cromwell followed King Charles II. into England, before the battle of Worceſter. He left General Monk to accompliſh the conqueſt of Scotland.

Scotland. This caſtle was then taken by him, when he carried the Scottiſh Records to London, they having been removed hither upon the ſurrender of Edinburgh Caſtle. In 1660 they were by King Charles II. packed up in hogſheads, and ſhipped for Scotland; but the ſhips being caſt away near Berwick, they were all irrecoverably loſt.

IN 1746 Stirling Caſtle was attacked by the Highlanders, but they were ſoon obliged to relinquiſh the ſiege.

THE area on which this caſtle ſtands is of an irregular figure, its length running nearly North and South, being double that of its breadth; it is divided into two courts.

THE entrance is on the South ſide, through a ſtrong gate, flanked by round towers; on the left, or Weſt, in a corner, ſtands the palace, a ſingular building, richly ornamented with grotesque figures.

PASSING the South Eaſt angle of the palace you come into a ſecond area, or kind of ſquare, where a little to the North Eaſt is the Old Parliament Houſe, a vaſt room, of one hundred and twenty feet long, very high, with a timbered roof: this building forms the Eaſt ſide of the ſquare. The North ſide is cloſed by the chapel; built by James VI. on the ſite of the collegiate one, as has been before obſerved.

THE Weſt ſide was bordered by a wall, beyond which, adjoining to the outward, or Weſtern wall of the caſtle, were the armory, and barracks for the garriſon; further Weſtward was the magazine.

ON the whole, the ſituation of this caſtle greatly reſembles that of Edinburgh, each being mounted on the ridge of a precipitous rock. This and the Caſtle of Dumbarton were ſaid jointly to ſecure the Lowlands from the incurſions of the Highlanders, the former as the Lock, of which Stirling was the Key.

THIS view was drawn A. D. 1790.

THE GREY FRIARS CHURCH, AT STIRLING.

THIS church was built A. D. 1494, by King James V. for a convent of Franciſcans or Grey Friars: it is a very handſome building, in the beſt ſtyle of what is called Gothic architecture: it is all of hewn ſtone,

with

with an arched roof, fupported by two rows of pillars. It was originally one church, but fince the Reformation has been divided by a partition wall, and at prefent makes two large and convenient places of worfhip, called the Eaft and Weft Church. A fmall addition to the Eaft end of the building is faid to have been made by Cardinal Beaton. This church is taken notice of in hiftory as the place where, in 1543, the Earl of Arran, Governor during the reign of Queen Mary, publickly renounced the Reformed Religion, which he had once profeffed to favour. It was alfo here that King James VI, was crowned in 1567.

DURING the fiege of the caftle by General Monk, in 1651, he raifed his batteries in this church yard. The fteeple and roof of the church have many marks of bullets, difcharged by the garrifon in their defence. Several fhots were alfo fired at this church, from the caftle, in the year 1746, when the Rebels ufed to fire fmall arms from the fteeple, and rang the bells to teftify their joy for the victory they had gained over the King's troops at Falkirk.

UPON the North fide of this church ftands a ruinous building, of good workmanfhip, called Marr's Work, having been erected by John, Earl of Marr, who was a fhort time Regent in the minority of James VI. The ftones with which it was built were brought from the Abbey of Cambufkenneth, the revenues of which were at that time held in commendam, by that Earl's near relations.

SUNDRY infcriptions, of no importance, are ftill legible * on the gate and other parts; upon the lintels of the doors and windows there

---

* On the gate of the tower, on the right of the entry:

The more I ftand in open height
My faults more fubject are to fight.

And over the great gate on the infide of the court:

Speak furth and fpare nocht;
Confider well I care nocht.

This is fuppofed to allude to the cenfures of the times on the Earl, for building this houfe out of the ftones of the diffolved Abbey of Cambufkenneth, of which he had been Prior, when a Clergyman.

are many ornaments; indeed there feems to have been a profufion of fculpture employed on the building. Many of the ftones have lately been carried away to build walls and other erections at the New Church Yard, at St. Ninian's; and what ftill remains of this fabric is preferved to protect the main ftreet or market-place from the fury of the Weftern winds. It is faid this manfion was never entirely completed.

Upon the right hand of the road leading to the caftle ftands a fpacious edifice, which once belonged to a noble family of the name of Alexander, which took the title of Earl from this town: it was afterwards in poffeffion of the family of Argyle, by whom it was lately fold. It is now confiderably out of repair, and let in different tenements. This view fhews the North fide of the church, with the gate of Lord Marr's houfe, drawn A. D. 1790, from the garden of the houfe laft defcribed, known by the appellation of the Lodgings.

PERTHSHIRE.

DOUN CASTLE.

THIS caftle, according to tradition, was built by Murdock, Duke of Albany, who was, it is faid, executed on a hill within fight of it.

IT is very pleafantly and ftrongly fituated, being almoft furrounded by the river Teath; for fize and ftrength it exceeds moft of the caftles in this part of Scotland, thofe of Edinburgh and Stirling excepted.

THE firft time it occurs in hiftory, is Sir James Stewart, of Beath, being appointed Conftable thereof by James V. The fon of this Sir James, in the year 1565, obtained a charter under the great feal of certain lands, to be called the Barony of Doun. He was a fteady friend to Queen Mary during the civil wars, when this caftle was always a fafe retreat to the loyalifts.

FORMERLY, before the abolition of hereditary offices, courts were held here, in a room kept in repair for that purpofe.

IN the Rebellion of the year 1745 it was for fome time occupied by the Rebels, who planted a twelve pounder in one of the windows, and feveral fwivels on the parapets; thefe guns were brought from a merchant fhip which had fallen into their hands.

ON its being quitted by the Rebels, an engineer was fent down by Government to furvey the caftle, with an intent to repair and fortify it, if capable of being made tenable; but it is probable that he reported to the contrary. It has fince been neglected and fuffered to fall to ruin. It is at prefent the property of the Earl of Murray.

THIS view was drawn A. D. 1790.

GOUT.

GOWRIE HOUSE OR CASTLE.

GOWRIE CASTLE stands on the South East side of the town of Perth, at the East end of the South-street. When, or by whom, it was built is not ascertained; but if one may judge from its appearance and style of architecture, it does not seem older than the time of James V. or at most his father, James IV.

It was the residence of the Earls of Gowrie, till forfeited by that noble family, on account of that strange and mysterious transaction, called Gowrie's Conspiracy, the scene of which was this house. The circumstances are too long and too intricate to b here properly related. Certain it is, that the attainder of this family caused very considerable escheats to the crown, and afforded the means of gratifying a number of rapacious courtiers.

After Lord Gowrie's forfeiture, the Magistrates obtained the property of this mansion or castle, which, in the year 1746, they presented, together with the freedom of the town, to his Royal Highness, William, Duke of Cumberland, from whom the Board of Ordnance, as report says, purchased it for five thousand pounds. It has ever since served as barracks for the detachment of the Royal Artillery, in Scotland.

THE MONKS TOWER.

This tower stands in a walk near the river Tay, in the garden of Gowrie House; it is of an oval figure, with a high roof, vaulted within; the area or internal measure is about twenty-four feet by thirteen; it has a fire-place and coved ceiling, in which are coarsely painted the twelve signs of the Zodiac, the Heathen Gods and Goddesses, and the arms, crest, and cyphers of the Hay family. The painting, from its style, does not seem older than the time of King Charles I. and is said to have been done by the same hand as the ceilings of the palace of Scoon. Apparently this tower was intended for a kind of fummer-houfe, or banquetting-room, the walls being by much too thin to have been built for the purpofe of defence.

Some have fuppofed this tower to have obtained the appellation of the Monks Tower from having, A. D. 1336, in obedience to the orders of King Edward, been built at the expence of the monafteries of Lindores, Balmarnock, Aberbrothick, and Coupar, in Angus; which expence, Fordun fays, in a manner ruined thofe monafteries; and adds, that John de Gowry, Prior of St. Andrew's, paid two hundred and eighty marks towards thefe works. This is in fome degree countenanced by Cant's notes to the Hiftory of Perth, in the following lines and note:

—— The great and ftrong Spey Towre
And Monks Towre builded round a wall of power.

Note. " The Spey Tower is gone; it was a ftately fortrefs, and had a ftrong prifon. The Roffes, of Cragie, were Governors of the fortrefs. At the Reformation Robert Rofs, of Cragie, delivered up the keys under a proteftation. There remains nothing of it but a pitiful ruin, where the toll-houfe is. Monks Tower yet ftands, as defcribed in the Poem, in the South Eaft corner of the garden, on the wall: it ferves for a magazine of gun-powder for the Train of Artillery. The wall between this and the Spey Tower is the wall of the garden, and the foffe without ftill remains." Perhaps this tower might have been erected on the fite of a more ancient one, and have taken its name from fome concern General Monk might have with it: but this is only conjecture, not founded on any authority.

HUNTING TOWER.

This was part of the poffeffions of the Gowrie family, and was originally called Ruthven Caftle; but being forfeited on account of the plot mentioned in the article of Gowrie, the name, to obliterate every trace of the family, was changed to that of Hunting tower. When, and by whom it was built, are equally unknown.

In this castle James VI. was, A. D. 1582, on his return from a hunting party in Athol, stopped by a number of his most faithful peers, with an intent to rescue him from his worthless favourites, who were poisoning his young mind, with arbitrary principles, under the specious appellation of the Royal Prerogative. The King endeavoured to escape, but was prevented, upon which bursting into tears, he was told by the Guardian of Glames, " That it was better children weep than bearded men." The confederated Lords carried the King off; but shortly after getting out of their hands, he put himself into the possession of Lord Arran. This transaction was called " The Raid of Ruthven."

Mr. Pennant mentions another remarkable, though more happy, event, which happened here: " A daughter of the first Earl of Gowrie was addressed by a young gentleman in the neighbourhood, much her inferior in rank and fortune; her family, though they gave no countenance to the match, permitted him to visit them, and lodged him in a tower, near another in which was the young lady's chamber, but up a different stair-case, and communicating with another part of the house: the lady, before the communicating doors were shut, conveyed herself into her lover's apartment; but some one of the family having discovered it, told it to her mother, who cutting off, as she thought, all possibility of retreat, hastened to surprise them; but the young lady, hearing the well-known footsteps of her mother hobbling up stairs, ran to the top of the leads, and took a desperate leap of nine feet four inches, over a chasm of sixty feet from the ground, lighted on the battlements of the other tower, whence descending into her own chamber, she crept into her bed; her mother having in vain sought her in her lover's chamber, came into her room, where finding her seemingly asleep, she apologized to her for her unjust suspicion. The young lady eloped the next night, and was married." The top of the towers, from and to which the lady leaped, are still shewn, under the appellation of the Maiden's Leap.

This castle consists of two ancient square towers, connected by buildings, of later date; it is still inhabited as a farm-house, though the back part is in ruins. The banquetting hall is still discoverable, the chimney of which is ornamented with grotesque heads of stucco; two of them in alto relievo, but much mutilated; the other two in baſſo relievo: they ſeem from their ſtyle about the time of James V.

This building, which is delightfully ſituated amidſt beautiful groves and plantations, belongs to the Duke of Athol; near it is a ſpring dedicated to St. Conwal, whoſe anniverſary is celebrated the 18th of May. It is ſaid, a late Duke of Athol took great delight in this place, and would have repaired it, but was prevented by a Dowager, on whom it was ſettled, who would not ſuffer any alterations to be made in it during her life.

This view, which ſhews the back part of the houſe and the banquetting hall, was drawn A. D. 1790.

ELCHO CASTLE.

This was a large and ſtrong caſtle: it ſtands near four miles below Perth, on the South ſide of the river Tay, about a mile below Kinfawns; it belongs to the Honourable Mr. Charters, of Ampsfield, ſecond ſon to the late Earl of Weems, and gives the title of Lord Elcho to the eldeſt ſon of that family. It is now in ruins, and has not been inhabited for many years. This view was drawn A. D. 1788.

CASTLE CAMPBELL. Plate I.

This caſtle, from its romantic ſituation, reſembles one of thoſe deſcribed in ancient romances, in which a cruel giant, aſſiſted by a pagan necromancer, kept confined, and enchanted, a number of captive Knights and Princeſſes.

Nothing can be more dreary than the ſcenes ſurrounding this building, which is ſeated on a ſteep peninſulated rock, between and under vaſt mountains, which overſhadow it, having to the South a view through a deep glen, ſhagged with bruſh-wood, and watered by a rivulet. From the dreary and ſolemn ſituation, this pile was formerly called the Caſtle of Gloom, and the names of the adjacent places ſeem to be analogous to it; for it stands in the Parish of Dolor, was bounded by the glen of Care, and washed by the burn of Sorrow.

Here is an extraordinary contrivance for procuring water under cover: a subterraneous way to the burn running at the bottom of the rock, on which the castle is situated, having been made with stone and lime, it is now broken at the top, and is to be seen through the bushes and brush-wood with which it is overgrown; looking down the conduit or steps affords a most tremendous sight. This castle, which with its circumscribing demesnes belonged to the Argyle family, was A. D. 1645 taken and burned by the Marquis of Montrose, who carried fire and sword through the whole estate. The landlord of the inn at Dolor said, his grandfather, who was agent to the Argyle family, put a roof on it. It was inhabited when the family were Marquisses of Lorn: at present it belongs to the Duke of Argyle.

This plate gives a near view of the castle.

CASTLE CAMPBELL. Plate II.

This view shews the castle at a distance, as seen from the village of Dolor. This and Plate I. were drawn A. D. 1790.

CULROSS, OR KYLLENROSS ABBEY.

This was a Cistertian Abbey, situated upon the Frith of Forth, in the shire of Perth, and diocese of Dumblane. It was founded in the year 1217 by Malcolm, Earl of Fife; the Chronicle of Melrofs, which records this foundation, says the monks and first abbot were sent from the abbey of Kinrofs. The conventual church was not only dedicated to the Virgin Mary, but also to St. Servanus the Confessor, whose festival was annually kept on the first day of July, even long after the Reformation; on which day the men and women were accustomed to assemble early in the morning, and walk in procession round the town, carrying green boughs in their hands, and afterwards
spending

spending the remainder of the day in feftivity. This proceffion is ftill continued, but is now changed from the Saint's day to the King's birth day.

A. D. 1489, John Hogg was abbot of this houfe; at which time, on the 14th of April, Culrofs was erected into a burgh of barony.

The laft abbot of this place was Alexander, fon to Sir James Colvil of Ochiltry. Sir James Colvil, brother to the faid Alexander, was by a patent, bearing date the 20th of January, 1709, * created a Peer by the title of Lord Colvil of Culrofs; at which time the King alfo granted to him this diffolved abbey.

It is faid that the Earls of Argyle, who in ancient times refided at Caftle Campbell, were heritable baillies of this abbey, which office they difpofed of to the Colvilles of Ochiltry, in whofe family it continued till thefe hereditable jurifdictions were abolifhed. The Argyle family had an aifle adjoining to the abbey church, in which they fometimes ufed to bury; the ruins of it are ftill vifible.

The abbey of Culrofs was placed on an elevation, commanding a beautiful and extenfive view of the Forth and the coaft on both fides. Confiderable remains of the monaftery are yet extant. The abbey church ftood on the North fide of it, and had a tower in the middle of it, which was in the year 1789 ftill entire, as was alfo the Weft part of the church, now ufed as a parochial kirk. The cloifter is ftill difcernible, and is now ufed by the minifter as a garden. On the Eaft and Weft fides were A. D. 1789, feveral remains of the offices of the houfe, particularly on the Weft fide, where there was a building, from its fize fuppofed to have been the refectory. Weft of this was the Abbot's Houfe; its walls were entire within the memory of perfons now living; at prefent they are nearly demolifhed.

In Keith's Appendix are the following particulars refpecting the revenues of this houfe:

Money 786l. 16s. 7¼d (Scots). Wheat 3 c. 3 b. Bear 15 c. 10 b. 2 f. Oats 13 c. 12 b. 3 f. 3½ p. Salt 1 c. 2 b. Wedders n. 10.

---

* See Douglas's Peerage.

Lambs n. 22. Capons 7 doz. Poultry 26½ d. Butter 7½ stone. Cheese 79½ stone. A. Straw 8 trusses. And the Abbot says, there were nine monks in the convent, five whereof had recanted; but the other four would not by any persuasion. And he mentions a certain allowance he had given to those that had recanted; but had given nothing to the others. This view was drawn 1784.

THE CATHEDRAL OF DUNBLANE.

THE Cathedral of Dunblane is situated on an eminence on the Eastern bank of the river Allan, and overlooking the town to which it probably gives name.

THE see of Dunblane was founded by King David, about the year 1142; he also built the cathedral.

ITS revenues at the Reformation amounted to the sum of 313l. (Scots) in money; 1 chaldron of wheat; 11 chaldron, 11 bolls, 3 firlots, and ¼ a peck of bear; 50 chaldron, 1 boll, 1 firlot, and 3½ pecks of meal; 9 chaldron and 12 bolls of oats. This church was once possessed of diverse lands in England.

MUCH of this cathedral is still standing, though fast falling to decay. The choir is kept in repair, and serves for the parochial church: under it are sepulchral vaults.

IN the choir are several of the oaken seats for the choristers, on which are carved, as usual, grotesque figures; among them, a cat, a fox, and an owl. At the upper end of the choir are some of the prebendaries stalls; on the right of the entrance the Bishop's seat, and on the left that of the Dean; these are also of oak handsomely carved.

HERE are several coarse blue marble stones over the graves of diverse of the bishops and Deans: on some of them there are the marks of brass plates.

BEHIND a modern seat is a niche in the wall, in which is the figure of a Bishop, as large as life; he is dressed in pontificalibus, with his mitre. The three steps to the altar still remain. In the niche where the vessel for holy water formerly stood, there is now a door.

The

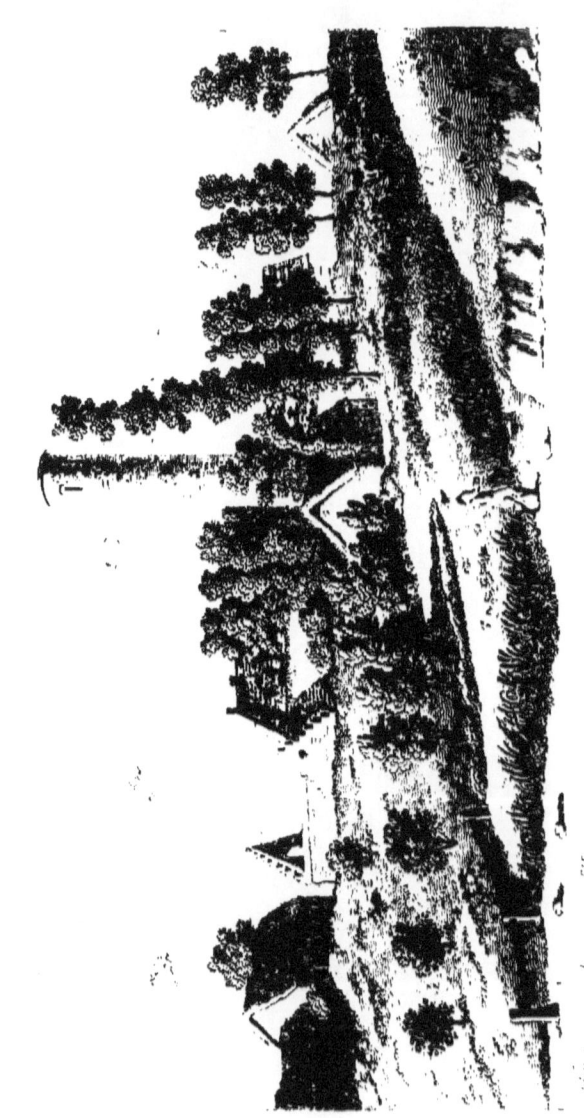

ABERNETHY TOWER, PL.

The families of Keir, Sticklings, Chifholms, Drummonds, and Fenlayfons have feparate places of burial here.

Some walls and other remains of the Bifhop's Palace are ftill vifible.

The length of this cathedral is 216 feet, breadth 76, height of the walls 50 feet, and of the tower 128 feet.

This view was drawn A. D. 1790.

ABERNETHY COLLEGE. Plate I.

ABERNETHY is fituated near the junction of the rivers Ern and Tay: it was once the capital city of the Picts. A collegiate church was built and founded here by Garnard Macdompnack, after which St. Brigid, a virgin of Caithnefs, was introduced by St. Patrick, with her nine virgins, who died within five years after their arrival, and were buried in the North part of the church. According to Spotfwood, St. Brigid died A. D. 518, and was alfo buried here.

Here was a bifhoprick, the metropolitan of all Scotland, till in the year 840, it was tranflated to St. Andrews, by Kenneth III. Here was alfo a convent of the Culdees, changed, A. D. 1272, to a priory of Canons Regular.

This place is moft remarkable for having one of thofe tall flender conical towers, of which there is only one more in Scotland, that is at Brechen, although they abound in Ireland; but their date, and the ufe for which they were conftructed, remains ftill doubtful, notwithftanding the refearches and inveftigations of antiquaries of different periods and nations.

By fome they have been deemed watch towers, for the purpofe of difcovering invaders at a diftance, and communicating by fignals their approach; others conceive them to have been belfries, introduced by fome of the crufaders, in imitation of the Minarets of Mofques, from whence the criers fummoned the people to prayers; and this they think receives fome countenance from the Culdees; the ancient religious order in Scotland being attached to the ceremonies of the Greek Church. Some have fuppofed them penitentiary towers, the refidence of a fort

of

of hermits, imitators of Simon Styllitis. All thefe conjectures are fupported, as ufual, by etymologies.

With refpect to the firft fuppofition, it is objected that they cannot have been meant for watch towers, fince they are not always placed on elevated ftations, commanding an uninterrupted profpect around them, but, on the contrary, are frequently covered by commanding hills, particularly towards that fide from whence danger was moft probable.

That they were imitations of Minarets, feems extremely improbable; the deteftation in which every article and circumftance of Pagan Worfhip was held by the Crufaders, makes it fcarcely poffible they would introduce any of them into the Chriftian Church. And for the argument deduced from the Culdees following the ceremonies of the Greek Church, it remains to be proved, that the Greeks ufed Minarets; befides it is generally held there were no Culdees in Ireland.

The third opinion, namely, that they were penitentiary towers, feems, on the whole, the moft prevalent, though it appears rather to have acquired the fuffrage from the defeat of its competitors, than from any very cogent reafons offered in its fupport.

Gordon vifited this tower, of which he gives the following account: " I went directly," fays he, " to Abernethy, the ancient capital of the Pictifh Nation, about four miles from Perth, to fee if I could find any remains of the Picts hereabouts; but could difcover nothing except a ftately hollow pillar, without a ftair-cafe; fo that when I entered within, and looked upward, I could fcarce forbear imagining myfelf at the bottom of a deep draw-well: it has only one door or entrance facing the North, fomewhat above the bafis, the height of which is eight foot and a half, and the breadth, from jamb to jamb, two and a half. Towards the top are four windows, which have ferved for the admiffion of light; they are equidiftant, and five feet nine inches in height, and two foot two inches in breadth, and each is fupported by two fmall pillars; at the bottom are two rows of ftones projecting from beneath, which ferved for the bafis of a pedeftal. The whole height of the pillar is feventy-five foot, and confifts of fixty-four rows, or regular courfes of hewn ftone: the external circumference at the bafe is forty-eight foot, but diminifhes fomewhat towards the

THE PRIORY, ABBEY'S REGULI.

the top; and the thicknefs of the wall is three foot and a half. This is, by the inhabitants hereabouts, called the Round Steeple of Abernethy; and is fuppofed to be the only remains of a Pictifh work in thefe parts." This view fhews the ruins of the church, with a diftant view of the tower.

ABERNETHY COLLEGE. Plate II.

This might, with more propriety, be called a view of the tower, of which it gives a particular delineation, as feen from the high road from Perth. Thefe views were drawn A. D. 1790.

ANGUSSHIRE.

GLAMES CASTLE. PLATE I.

GLAMES Castle originally consisted of two rectangular towers, longer than broad, with walls of fifteen feet in thickness; they were connected by a square projection, and together formed a figure somewhat like the letter Z, saving that in the castle all the angles were right ones. This form gave mutual defences to part of the building.

GREAT alterations and additions were made to this house by Patrick, Earl of Kinghorn; these, according to the above cited plan, a date carved on a stone on the outside of the building, and other authorities, were done in the year 1606, and not 1686, as is said in an ancient print, engraved about that time. The architect employed on this occasion, as tradition reports, was Inigo Jones; indeed the work seems greatly to resemble Herriot's Hospital, at Edinburgh, and diverse other buildings designed by him. The great hall was finished A. D. 1621. It is a handsome room, with a coved ceiling, adorned with heads and ornaments in stucco. Here are many family portraits, among them a large picture in a carved oaken frame, representing Earl Patrick and his Three Sons. In the back ground a view of the castle, as it was in 1683. At that time there were three gates leading from the park. In the ancient part of this castle is shewed the room wherein Malcolm II. was murdered. Fordun has it, that he was killed at or near the town of Glames; but does not say in the castle.

A PARTICULAR description is given of this mansion in an Anonymous Journey through Scotland, published in 1723. Since which diverse alterations have been projected in the building, for which one of the wings has been partly pulled down, and is not yet rebuilt.

."IN

"In the entering Strathmore I arrived at the noble palace of Glames, belonging to Lion, Earl of Strathmore. This palace, as you approach it, first awes you with awe and admiration, by the many turrets and gilded balluftrades at the top. It ftands in the middle of a well planted park, with avenues cut through every way to the houfe. The great avenue thickly planted on each fide, at the entrance of which there is a great ftone gate, with offices on each fide, of free ftone, like a little town, leads you in haif a mile to the outer court, which has a ftatue on each fide, on the top of the gate, as big as the life. On the great gate of the inner court are balluftrades of ftone finely adorned with ftatues; and in the court are four brazen ftatues, bigger than the life, on pedeftals; the one of James VI. and firft of England in his ftole; the other of Charles I. in his boots, fpurs, and fword, as he is fometimes painted by Vandyke; Charles II. is in a Roman drefs, as on the Exchange, in London; and James II. in the fame he is in at Whitehall. From this court by balluftrades of iron you have a full profpect of the gardens on each fide, cut into grafs plats, and adorned with ever-greens, which are very well kept. The houfe is the higheft I ever faw, confifting of a high tower in the middle, with two wings, and a tower at each end; the whole above two hundred feet broad. The ftairs from the entry to the top of the houfe confifts of one hundred and forty-three fteps, of which the great ftairs, where five people can mount abreaft, are eighty-fix, each of one ftone. In the firft floor are thirty-eight fire rooms. The hall is adorned with family pictures; and behind the hall is a handfome chapel, with an organ, for the church of England fervice. On the altar is a good picture of the Laft Supper, and on the ceiling an Afcenfion, done by one De Wit, a Dutchman, whom Earl Patrick, this Earl's Grandfather, brought from Holland, and who painted the ceilings of moft of the rooms.

In the drawing room, next to the hall, is the beft picture I ever faw, of Queen Mary of Modena, the Pretender's mother. The Duke of Lauderdale in his robes, by Sir Peter Lely; and the late Lord Dundee, with a crowd of half lengths of the nobility of Scotland; and over a chimney a curious Italian piece, of our Saviour difputing with the Doctors in the Temple.

When the Pretender lay here they made eighty-eight beds, within the houfe, for him and his retinue, befides the inferior fervants, who lay in the offices out of doors. The prefent Earl's elder brother faved the eftate from being forfeited by being killed at the head of his regiment, on Shiremore."

In the court before the minifter's houfe is fhewn a ftone, on which is engraved a crofs and diverfe figures, faid to allude to the murder of King Malcolm, and the deaths of the murderers, who attempting to crofs the lake of Forfar, then flightly frozen over, the ice broke, and they were drowned.—This ftone is defcribed and engraved in Mr. Pennant's Tour. Diverfe weapons, with fome brafs veffels lately found in draining that lake, are fhewn in the caftle.

The tradition of an ancient lofty building, called the Tower of Glamis, fituated on an eminence near the center of the town of Kinghorn, in Fifefhire, is ftill preferved in that place. It ferved as a fea-mark to failors navigating the Forth. This building becoming ruinous, a gentleman in the neighbourhood obtained leave of the Strathmore family, to whom it belonged, to take the ftones for the purpofe of building, on condition that he fhould put down a pillar on the fpot whence he took the ftones, with this infcription, " Here ftood Glamis Tower." This pillar is remembered by many of the inhabitants at prefent (A. D. 1789) living; but it is now removed.

This view was drawn A. D. 1790.

GLAMES CASTLE. Plate II.

This view gives a more picturefque, though lefs defcriptive, delineation of the caftle than the former. They were both drawn on the fame day.

ABERBROTH ABBEY.

Aberbroth, or Aberbrothack, in the Shire of Angus, is fituated on the fea fhore, on the burn of Brithock or Brothe. It was

one

ANGUSSHIRE.

one of the richeft and moft fumptuous abbeys in Scotland, and was founded, A. D. 1178, by King William the Lion, who was buried here. It was dedicated to St. Thomas Becket, Archbifhop of Canterbury, and filled with Benedictine or Tyronefian Monks, brought from the Abbey of Kelfo.

THIS place is in feveral manufcripts called Monafterium Bajocenfe, and by Dempfter Aberbredock-kuidel. King Robert Bruce granted to this abbey ten marks fterling, to be received annually from the Thanage of Monifoth, for maintaining lights about the tomb of William, King of Scotland; and King John, of England, probably out of regard to the monaftery, granted to the inhabitants of this town the privilege of difpofing of their goods any where within his dominions, London excepted, toll and cuftom free. Pope Lucius III. in the year 1182, confirmed all donations that were made to this monaftery.

THE firft Abbot was Reginaldus, a Monk of Tyron, who was, in the year 1178, releafed by John Abbot of Kelfo, from all fubordination due to him as Abbot of that monaftery; to which charter Richard, of Aburbuthenoth or Arbuthnot, the King's Clerk, was witnefs: this Reginaldus was confecrated at King William's requeft, by Mathew, Bifhop of Aberdeen, the church of St. Andrew being then vacant.

THE fecond Abbot was Henry, a profeffed Monk of Kelfo, who was likewife, A. D. 1179, releafed by the Abbot of that houfe, from that fubjection to him and his fucceffors, which he had at his profeffion fworn to obferve.

BERNARD, Abbot of Aberbroth, was Chancellor under King Robert Bruce, and afterwards Bifhop of the Ifles. May 2d, 1394, an indenture was made between John Geddy, Abbot of this houfe, and the burgeffes of the town, whereby that Abbot, for certain confiderations, obliges himfelf and his fucceffors, at their proper expence and charges, to maintain the pier in fuch ftate that veffels may enter, and lay there in fafety.

IN the year 1461 Pope Pius II. granted the Abbot of this houfe an exemption from attending at the yearly epifcopal fynods, of which he directed the Bifhop of St. Andrew's to give notice to his brethren, threatening excommunication to any one who fhould trouble him on-that account. Yet it does not appear (fays Keith) that thefe threats were regarded by John Bifhop of Brechin, and Alexander Bifhop of Murray.

Pope Benedict, by his Bull, dated at Avignon, 6 Kal. June, and the fecond year of his Pontificate, granted to John, Abbot of Aberbroth, and his fucceffors, the privilege of making ufe of and wearing the mitre, ring, robes, and other Epifcopal Infignia; and Pope Martin, by his Bull of the 5th Id. June, and the third of his Pontificate, authorifed Walter, Abbot thereof, and his fucceffors, to confer the minor orders on the Monks and Clerks of their convent.

The laft Ecclefiaftic Abbot was Cardinal Beaton, at the fame time Archbifhop of St. Andrew's.

The laft Commendatory Abbot of this houfe was John Hamilton, fecond fon to the Duke of Chaftelherault, afterwards created Marquis of Hamilton. This Abbey was erected into a temporal lordfhip, in favour of James, Marquis of Hamilton, fon to the former; the grant is dated upon the 5th of May, 1608.

This Abbey afterwards belonged to the Earl of Dyfart, from whom it was purchafed, with the right of patronage of thirty-four parifh churches, belonging to it, by Patrick Maule, of Panmure, Gentleman of the Bed Chamber to King James VI. in which family it remained till the year 1715, when it efcheated to the crown by forfeiture, and was under the management of the Barons of the Exchequer. A. D. 1752 part of the fite of the Abbey was obtained by the town.

For the adminiftration of juftice the Convent elected and paid an officer, called Bailey of the Regality, which became hereditary; the family of Airly held it before the Reformation, and till the year 1747, when it was fold and vefted in the crown, with other hereditable jurifdictions. The walls of the Regality Prifon are ftill remaining.

In the year 1445 the election of this officer proved fatal to the Chieftains of two noble families: the Convent had that year chofen Alexander Lindefay, eldeft fon of the Earl of Crawford, to be Judge or Bailey of their Regality; but he proved fo expenfive by his number of followers, and high way of living, that they were obliged to remove him, and appoint in his place Alexander, nephew to John Ogilvie, of Airly, who had an hereditary claim to the place: this occafioned a

cruel

cruel feud between the families; each affembled their vaffals, and terminated the difpute near the town: the Lindefays were victorious; but both the principals fell in the battle, with about five hundred of their followers.

THE ordinance for the yearly provifion of the houfe in 1530, will give fome idea of its hofpitality and charity: there was an order for buying 800 wethers, 180 oxen, 11 barrels of falmon, 1200 dried codfifh, 82 chalders of malt, 30 of wheat, 40 of meal. All which appears additional to the produce of their lands, or the provifion of different fpecies paid in kind by their tenants.

THIS profufion of ftores would appear very extraordinary, as the number of Monks did not exceed twenty-five; but the ordinance acquaints us, that the appointments of that year exceeded thofe of 1528, notwithftanding, in the laft, the King had been entertained twice in the Convent, and the Archbifhop thrice: from this it is evident that the houfe was open to all; that the great as well as the poor partook of it, and that it was rather increafing than diminifhing.

THE following ftate of the revenues of this houfe is given in Keith's Appendix. The Collector's Book:

" MONEY 2483l. 5s. (Scots.) Wheat 26 chalders, 9 bolls, 1 firlot. Bear 118 c. 7 b. 2 p. Meal 168 c. 8 b. 2 f. Oats 27 c. 10 b. 3 f. 3½. Salmon 1 laft 3 barrels. The Book of Affumption makes it, Money 2555l. 14s. (Scots.) Wheat 30 c. 3 b. 3 f. 2 p. Bear 143 c. 9 b. 2 p. Meal 296 c. 9 b. 2 1. Oats 27 c. 11 b. Salmon 3 laft 1 barrel. Omitted capons, poultry, graffumes dawikis, and all other fervices, and fmall dewties. Alfo a N. B. that the Xirkis of Abernethy and Monyfuith are nocht comptit, herein."

IN another part of this book a like rental is given in the Latin tongue, foon after the year 1561, in which, befides 37 barrels of falmon, are contained likewife 2 barrels of Glyffart (Grifles f. i. e. young falmon.) To this Latin Rental is added, the Valuation of the Kirks of Abernethy, Manyfuith, and Tanadies, viz. Abern. 273l. Tan. 237l. 5s. 4d. Manyf. ol. os. od. Wheat 4 c. 12 b. Bear 12 c. 9 b. Meal 15 c. 13 b. None of all which is put in the Rental. In the furplus of the third book, money 1594l. in the other articles it agre e

with

with the firſt ſtatement, except in the ſalmon, which is the ſame as the ſecond.

This Abbey was built with a red ſtone found hereabouts, which ill reſiſts the weather, ſo that the ornamented parts expoſed to the open air, are much defaced, and the carvings ſcarcely diſtinguiſhable. The buildings of this houſe were all encloſed by a ſtrong wall, the ground forming an irregular figure. The length from North to South about one hundred and ninety geometrical paces, and the mean breadth, from Eaſt to Weſt one hundred and thirteen; the breadth at the North end exceeding that at the South upwards of one third.

On the South Weſt corner is a tower, now the ſteeple of the preſent pariſh Kirk; and at the South Eaſt corner is the darn, or private gate, over which was a houſe for catechiſing. The greateſt part of the walls were ſtanding within the memory of man, but are now nearly demoliſhed.

On the North ſide of the area, and almoſt in the middle, between the two corners, ſtood the Abbey Church, which was of the figure of a croſs. Weſt of the tranſept it was divided into a middle and two ſide aiſles, by a double row of columns, ſupporting arches. The meaſures of this church are as follows:

Inside length of the whole church, from Eaſt to Weſt, 270 feet.

Breadth of the middle aiſle 35 feet; ſide aiſles each $16\frac{1}{2}$ feet. Total breadth of the whole church, ſide aiſles included, 68 feet.

Length from the Weſt end to the tranſept 148 feet. Breadth of the tranſept, ſide aiſle of $16\frac{1}{2}$ feet included, $45\frac{1}{2}$ feet.

Length of the whole tranſept, from North to South, 132 feet.

Length from the Eaſt end to the tranſept $76\frac{1}{2}$ feet.

The height of the ſide walls, as appears from the mark of the roof on the ruins, was about 67 feet.

Part of the Abbot's houſe is ſtill ſtanding, and inhabited; in here ſome of the ancient floors are remaining, and ſeveral handſome carvings in oak. This Abbey, on the whole, though not the moſt elegant when entire, yet from the magnitude of its parts, is the moſt magnificent in Scotland.

This view was drawn a. d. 1788.

ABERBROTH ABBEY. Plate II.

THIS view, which shews the outside of the great gate, with the Regality Prison, was drawn, A. D. 1790.

THE CATHEDRAL CHURCH OF BRECHEN.

BRECHEN was a Bishop's see. It was founded about the year 1140, by King David I. Its annual revenues, in money and rents paid in kind, before the Reformation, are said to have amounted to seven hundred pounds; but, after that event, were diminished to one hundred and fifty, owing to alienations of its estates, made by Alexander Campbell, the first Protestant Bishop, to his Chieftain, the Earl of Argyle, by whose interest he had been promoted to that see. Keith in his Appendix says, " In this Bishoprick there is great confusion and uncertainty."

THE Culdees had a Convent here, which afterwards gave way to the Mathurines, or Red Friars: but neither of them seem to have had any thing to do with this church. The ruins of the Abbey of Red Friars, called the College, according to Maitland, are yet to be seen in the College Wynd, adjoining to the North Western end of the Grammar School.

THIS Church is a handsome building, in length one hundred and sixty feet, in breadth sixty-one; the Eastern part is ruinous; the Western part now serves for the parish church. Round it, under the eaves of the roof, ran a handsome cornice, carved, with quatrefoils and brackets.

THE tower is an hundred and twenty feet high, square, and embattled, having four small chinks or windows over each other, above which are the belfry windows, large, with pointed arches, divided into two by a mullion, which separates at the top, and give spaces for a handsome quatrefeuil. This tower is crowned with an hexagonal spire, pierced with small windows.

THERE is another tall slender tower, similar to that at Abernethy: Gordun describes it in his Itinerary, in the following words: "In my journey Northward I found a steeple at Brechen, differing little in shape from that at Abernethy, only it was larger, and covered at the top; for its height from the base to the cornice is eighty-five feet, and from thence to the vane fifteen, in all one hundred; it consists of sixty regular courses of stone; the external circumference thereof is forty-seven feet, and the thickness of the wall three feet eight inches; however this has no pedestal like the other, but seems to shoot out of the ground like a tree; it has a door fronting the South, the height and breadth of which differs little from Abernethy; only upon it are evidences sufficient to demonstrate that it was a Christian work, for over the top of the door is the figure of our Saviour on the Cross, with two little images or statues towards the middle.

THIS steeple has a low spiral roof of stone, with three or four windows above the cornice, and on the top there is placed a vane; it has no staircase within any more than the other; but the inhabitants of both towns ascend to the top by ladders: the vulgar notion of these is, that they are Pictish; and I should easily have rested in that opinion, had I not been since that time assured that some of the like monuments are to be seen in Ireland, where the Picts never settled." These measures differ somewhat from Mr. Pennant's; he says, "the height from the ground is eighty feet; the inner diameter, within a few feet of the bottom, is eight feet; the thickness of the walls at that part seven feet two inches; so that the whole diameter is fifteen feet two; the circumference very near forty-eight feet; the inner diameter at the top is seven feet eight inches; the thickness of the walls four feet six; the circumference thirty-eight feet eight inches; which proportion gives the building an inexpressible elegance: the top is roofed with an octagonal spire, twenty-three feet high, which makes the whole one hundred and three feet high; in this spire are four windows placed alternate on the sides, resting on the top of the tower: near the top of the tower are four others facing the four cardinal points." A mason, who was at work on the church when I saw it, said he had measured this tower for a wager, and found its height to the top of

the

the vane to be one hundred and eight feet exactly. In describing the male figure under the Crucifix, Mr. Pennant thinks it was meant for St. John; to me it appeared to have a large beard, and to be leaning on a kind of crutch; whereas St. John is always represented as a handsome young man. The tower is connected to the church by a small covered passage. There are at present two bells in this tower, to which the ascent is by ladders. This view, which shews the North East aspect of the church, was drawn A. D. 1790.

THE RED CASTLE.

This Castle stands on a high cliff, called the Red Head, on the South side of the Bay Lunan. It probably took its denomination of the Red Castle, from the colour of the cliff whereon it is built, which is red, as are also the stones used in its construction, like those of the Abbey of Aberbroth.

This, according to tradition, was once the residence of King William, surnamed the Lion, by whom it is likewise said to have been built. He began his reign in the year 1165, and died in 1214. Very little of this castle is at present remaining, as may be seen by the view. Its ragged fragments carry the appearance of antiquity.

In Haddington's Chart, p. 583, there is an entry of a charter granted by King Robert de Bruce, to Sir Donald Campbell, of the moiety of the Barony of Red Castle, which Henry de Percy, Knight, had forfeited to that King. Whether this castle is meant or not I will not take upon me to determine. This view was drawn A. D. 1790.

RESTENNOTE PRIORY.

The description of this Priory is given in that of Jedburgh, in Tiviotdale, to which it was a cell.

ABERDEENSHIRE.

THE CATHEDRAL CHURCH, OLD ABERDEEN.

THIS Bishoprick was originally founded at Murthlack, in the county of Banff, by Malcolm II. in the year 1010, in commemoration of a great victory obtained by him over the Danes. Beanus was by him appointed Bishop thereof; he was the first Scotch Prelate that had a Diocese assigned to him.

THIS See having continued one hundred and twenty-seven years at Murthlack, was, in the year 1137, translated to Aberdeen by King David I. who confirmed to it the lands of Murthlack, Cloveth, and Dunmeth.

MATHEW KENNIMOUTH, the third Bishop after the translation to Aberdeen, and who succeeded about the year 1165, began this Cathedral, which was dedicated to St. Marchar: whether it was finished during his life time or not is uncertain.

HENRY CHEEN, the twelfth Bishop, who died 1329, repaired this building, which had suffered much during the contention between Bruce and Bailiol.

ALEXANDER KENNIMOUTH, the second Bishop of that name, the sixteenth after the translation of the See, succeeded about the year 1356. He not thinking the church sufficiently beautiful for a Cathedral, caused it to be pulled down, and laid the foundation of one more magnificent; but before the work was advanced six cubits high, he was sent out of the land by the King, on an embassy, and died soon after his return.

ABOUT the year 1340 the English set fire to the town of Aberdeen, which burned six days, when the Bishop's Palace, and all the Prebendal Houses, were destroyed.

THE

ABERDEENSHIRE.

The Cathedral appears to have remained unfinished till the accession of Bishop Henry Leighton, in the year 1424, who greatly advanced that work, and bestowed large sums of his own for perfecting it; he built also a chapel within it, called St. John's chapel, in which he was buried about the year 1441.

Bishop Thomas Spence, who died 1480, greatly adorned this Cathedral, and rebuilt the Bishop's Palace, &c. which had remained in ruins ever since the burning thereof by the English.

Bishop William Elphinstone, who died in 1514, proposed great additions to this church; he began the choir and East end of it, but did not live to complete his plan.

Bishop Gawen Dunbar, who died in 1531, set himself to perfect what Bishop Elphinstone had begun, and therefore sued the Bishop's executors for certain Legacies left by that Prelate for those purposes, adding thereto money of his own; but the Reformation hindered the completion; this building suffered much by that event, but more, it is said, by the Revolution.*

---

* This venerable pile, which had suffered so much by the Reformation, did not escape the fury of the Covenanters, in the unfortunate reign of King Charles I. So violent was the zeal of that reforming period against all monuments of idolatry, that, perhaps, the Sun and Moon, very antient objects of false worship, owed their safety to their distance. As there was then nothing to be found worth carrying off, the illiberal zealots wreaked their vengeance upon the stones and timber. The high altar-piece, of the finest workmanship of any thing of that kind in Europe, had to that time remained inviolate; but in the year 1649 was hewed to pieces by order, and with the aid, of the parish Minister. The carpenter employed for this infamous purpose, awed by the sanctity of the place, and struck with the noble workmanship, refused to lay a tool on it, till the more than Gothic Priest took the hatchet from his hand, and struck the first blow. The wainscoting was richly carved, and ornamented with different kinds of crowns at the top, admirably cut: one of these, large, and of superior workmanship, even staggered the zeal of the furious Priest; he wished to save it, perhaps as a trophy over a fallen enemy; whatever his motive may have been, his hopes were disappointed; while the carpenter rudely hewed down the supporting timbers, the crown fell from a great height, plowed up the pavement of the church, and flew in a thousand pieces.—Douglas's Description of the East Coast of Scotland. In his account the dates respecting the accessions of the Bishops, repairs, &c. differ widely from Spotswood, whose Chronology has been here adopted.

HERE was a grand crofs aifle from South to North, and a fine tower, which fell down in the year 1688, having been undermined by Oliver Cromwell's foldiers, for ftones to build a fort; by its fall the reft of the church was much damaged.

OF this ancient building, there at prefent remains the two fpires, one hundred and twelve feet high, and the nave, one hundred and thirty-five by fixty-four feet, infide meafure. It has a handfome window at the Weft end, and on the board cieling are painted in three columns forty-eight armorial bearings.

THE revenues of this Bifhoprick were in the year 1562, in money 1653l. 16s. 9d. (Scots); 3 chaldrons and 8 bolls of wheat; 35 chaldrons, 8 bolls, 3 firlots, and 3¼ pecks of bear; 24 chaldrons, 4 bolls, 2 firlots of meal, 8 chaldrons, 2 bolls, 3 firlots, and 2 pecks of oats; 46 mairts; 141 muttons; 121 wethers; 65¼ dozen of capons; 119 dozen of poultry; 55 geefe; 19 dozen of moor-fowls; 17 fwine; 12 lafts and 10 barrels of falmon.

KINCARDINESHIRE.

DUNOTTER CASTLE.

Dunotter Castle is situated on the East coast of Kincardineshire, on a rock projecting into the sea, acceffible from the land on the West side, and that only by a narrow, steep, and winding path over a deep gully, by which it is connected with the main land, and which ferves as a kind of natural fofs or ditch, the adjacent rock having been fcarped, and rendered inacceffible by art.

The entrance into the castle is through a gate, in a wall of about forty feet high, whence, by a long paffage, partly arched over, and through another gate pierced with four oilliets or loop-holes, you enter the area of the castle, which meafures about an English acre and a quarter. This paffage was also formerly ftrengthened by two iron portcullifes.

This area is furrounded by an embattled wall, and occupied by buildings of very different ages. The oldeft except the chapel is a fquare tower, faid to have been built about the latter end of the fourteenth century. A large range of lodging rooms and offices, with a long gallery, of one hundred and twenty feet, feems of a very modern date, not older than the latter end of the fixteenth century.

Here are also fhewn the ruins of diverfe other buildings, and conveniences neceffary for a garrifon; fuch as a chapel, barracks, a bafon, or ciftern of water, twenty feet diameter, a bowling green, and a forge, faid to be ufed for cafting iron bullets.

On this rock, notwithftanding its difficulty of accefs, the church and burial place of the parifh was originally fituated. The building now called the chapel, being formerly the parifh church. During the contention between Bruce and Baliol, the natural ftrength of this rock

induced

induced Sir William Keith, then Great Marifchal of Scotland, to build a caftle on it, as a place of fafety for himfelf and friends, during thofe troublefome times; but, in order to avoid offence, he firft built a church for the parifh in a more convenient place, notwithftanding which the Bifhop of St. Andrew's pronounced fentence of excommunication againft him, for violating facred ground. Sir William, on this, applied to Pope Benedict XIII. fetting forth the exigency of the cafe, and the neceffity of fuch a fortrefs, with the circumftances of his having built another church: on which his holinefs iffued his Bull, dated July 18, 1394, directing the Bifhop to take off the excommunication, and to allow Sir William to enjoy the caftle at all times, on the payment of a certain recompence to the church; fince which it has continued in the Keith family till the forfeiture of the late Earl, in 1715.

Mr. PENNANT, from Crawford's Peerage, fays, "the property of the Keiths, in this country, came to them in the reign of David Bruce, by the marriage of Sir William to Margaret, daughter of Sir John Frafer: but I have been informed that this fortrefs had been the property of an Earl of Crawford, who exchanged it for an eftate in Fife, with an Earl Marifchal, on condition that he and his dependants fhould, in cafe of neceffity, be permitted to take refuge there."

ABOUT the year 1296 this caftle was taken by Sir William Wallace, who, according to his hiftorian, burnt four thoufand Englifhmen in it; he fays:

> The Englifhmen that durft them not abide
> Before the hoft full fear'dly forth they flie
> To Dunnoter, a fwake within the fea.
> No further they might win out of the land,
> They fembled there while they were four thoufand
> Ran to the Kirk, ween'd girth to have tane,
> The Lave remained upon the Rock of Stane.
> The Bifhop then began treaty to ma,
> Their lives to get, out of the land to ga;
> But they were rude, and durft not well affy:
> Wallace in fire gart fet all haftily,
>   Burnt

KINCARDINESHIRE.

Burnt up the Kirk and all that was therein,
Attour the rock, the lave ran with great din,
Some hung on crags right dolefully to die,
Some lap, fome fell, fome fluttered in the Sea,
No *Southeron* in life was left in that hold,
And them within they burnt to powder cold.
When this was done, feil fell on their knees down,
At the Bifhop afk'd abfolution.
When Wallace leugh, faid, I forgive you all,
Are ye war-men, repent you for fo fmall?
They rued us not into the town of Air,
Our true barons when they hanged there.

IN 1336 this caftle was refortified by King Edward III. in his progrefs through Scotland: but was, as foon as that king quitted the kingdom, retaken by the Guardian, Sir Andrew Murray.

NOTHING refpecting this caftle occurs in hiftory, till the civil wars of the laft century, when it was befieged by the Marqui of Montrofe, and the church again burned.

THIS caftle was inhabited till the beginning of the prefent century; but was demolifhed foon after its forfeiture, in the year 1715, when its ruins were repurchafed by the Earl, and afterwards fold by him to Mr. Keith of Rovelfton. The Annotator of Camden mentions the ftately rooms in the new buildings and the library; he alfo fpeaks of St. Padie's Church, here famous for being the burial place of St. Palladius, who, in 431, was fent by Pope Celeftine to preach the Gofpel to the Scots.

IN this caftle, during Cromwell's Ufurpation, the Regalia of Scotland, confifting of the crown, fword, and fceptre, were depofited; the Earl being then appointed, by King Charles II. one of the Commiffioners for managing the government while his Majefty was abroad. Mr. Ogilvie, to whom the defence of this caftle was committed, finding it fo clofely invefted that he could not long hold out, prevailed on the wife of the Minifter of Kineef, a bold and prudent woman, who happened to be in the caftle at that time, to affift in conveying them away; this ſhe did by packing them up in a bundle, as things of no value, and walking boldly out with them. They were afterwards hid under the pulpit of Kineef, till the Reſtoration. This eſcape ſucceeded the more eaſily, as Mr. J Keith, who, on the caſtle being inveſted, ſailed immediately for France, had induſtriouſly cauſed it to be reported that he had taken them with him. For this piece of ſervice the King, at his Reſtoration, created Sir William Keith, Knight Mariſchal of Scotland, and Earl of Kintore. The caſtle was at the time of the above-mentioned ſiege well ſtored with cannon and ammunition. On the ſurrender the enemy allowed the iron guns and four mortars to remain; but carried off the reſt, viz. twenty-one braſs cannon, one hundred and forty fixed muſkets, and many firelocks, twenty-ſix barrels of powder, and ten cheſts of muſket balls.

This view was drawn A. D. 1790.

BANFF-

BANFFSHIRE.

BOYNE CASTLE. Plate I.

This Castle stands about six miles South of Cullen; it is romantically situated on a high perpendicular rock, on the South side of a deep gloomy ravine or glen, through which runs the river. The banks are wooded quite to the waters edge.

This was the Baronial Castle of the district called the Boyne, and anciently the residence of the family of the Ogilvies, ancestors of the present noble proprietor, Lord Findlater.

The building does not appear to have been very large, nor could it ever have been long tenable against besiegers, being commanded on the South side by a hill, which runs quite to its walls, looking down into it.

The castle was in figure a rectangular parallelogram, its angles flanked by round towers. The grand entrance was on the South side, over a draw-bridge, and through a gate, defended also by two round towers. It is now quite a ruin, as the views sufficiently shew. It was lately used for a granary.

This view shews the front or South side, with the gate or chief entrance. It was drawn A. D. 1790.

BOYNE CASTLE. Plate II.

This shews the North side of the building, with the rock and river. It was drawn A. D. 1790.

THE

THE CASTLE OF INCHDREWR.

This was the caftle of the Barony of Inchdrewr, in the county of Banff; it is fituated at a fmall diftance from the sea, and by the ftyle of its architecture feems to have been built about the time of King James IV. or V.

SIR GEORGE OGILVY, of Dunlugas, who was created a Baronet by King Charles I. on 10th of July, 1627, in the fame year, obtained a charter under the great feal, of the lands of the Barony of Inchdrewr. He was afterwards raifed to the dignity of Peerage, by the title of Lord Ogilvie, of Banff, by letters patent to him and the heirs male of his body, dated 31ft of Auguft, 1642.

MORAYSHIRE.

THE CATHEDRAL CHURCH OF ELGIN.

This was the Cathedral Church of the Diocese of Moray, translated from the Church of the Holy Trinity, at Spynie, at the request of the Chapter and King Alexander II. and by virtue of a bull from Pope Honorius, dated 10th April, 1224.

It appears that here was a church before the translation, which probably was taken down as soon as the new one was finished, as being too mean for a Cathedral. Bishop Andrew Moray is said to have laid the foundation stone of the new Cathedral Church on the very day on which the translation was declared, viz. 19th July, 1224.

After this church had stood one hundred and sixty-six years, from the date of its foundation, it was burned down in the year 1390, by Alexander Stewart, Lord of Badenoch, commonly called the Wolf of Badenoch, son of King Robert II. for which he was excommunicated; but on making due submission and reparation, was again received into the church.

Bishop Barr began rebuilding the church, and every Canon contributed. Bishop Spynie continued the work; but though every parish paid a subsidy, yet through the troubles of the times, it made slow advances. Bishop Innes laid the foundation of the great steeple, in the middle of the church, and greatly advanced it. After his death the Chapter met, May 18, 1414, and bound themselves, by a solemn oath, that whosoever should be elected Bishop, he should annually apply one third of his revenue to the rebuilding the Cathedral, until it should be finished.

THE church at length being rebuilt, it remained entire for many years, till in the beginning of the fixteenth century, about the year 1506, the great fteeple in the center fell down; the next year Bifhop Foreman began to rebuild it; but the work was not finifhed before the year 1538, when the height of the tower, including the fpire, was one hundred and ninety-eight feet.

THIS church, (fays Shaw) when entire, was a building of Gothic architecture, inferior to few in Europe; it ftood due Eaft and Weft, in the form of a Paffion or Jerufalem Crofs, ornamented with five towers, whereof two parallel ftood on the Weft end, one in the middle, and two on the Eaft end; betwixt the two towers on the Weft end was the great porch or entrance. This gate is a concave arch, twenty-four feet broad, in bafe, and twenty-four in height, terminating in a fharp angle. On each fide of the doors, in the fweep of the arch, are eight round and eight fluted pilafters, fix and a half feet high, adorned with a chapiter, from which arife fixteen pilafters, which meet in the key of the arch. There were porticoes, or to-falls on each fide of the church, Eaftwards, from the traverfe or crofs, which were eighteen feet broad without the walls. To yield fufficient light to a building fo large, befides the great windows in the porticoes and a row of attic windows in the walls, each fix feet high, above the porticoes, there was, in the Weft gable, above the gate, a window in form of an acute angled arch, nineteen feet broad in bafe, and twenty feven in height; and in the Eaft gable, between the turrets, a row of fine parallel windows, each two feet broad, and ten high; above thefe are five more, each feven feet high; and over all a circular window, near ten feet in diameter. In the heart of the wall of the church, and leading to all the upper windows, there is a channel or walk round the whole building.

THE grand gate, the windows, the pillars, the projecting table, pedeftals, cordons, &c. are adorned with foliage, grapes, and other carving. Let us, after defcribing the body of the church, take a view of the Chapter Houfe, commonly called " the Apprentices Ifle," a curious piece of architecture, ftanding on the North fide of the church, and communicating with the choir by a vaulted veftry. The houfe is an exact octagon, thirty-four feet high; and the diagonal breadth,

within

within the walls, thirty-feven feet. It is arched and vaulted at the top, and the whole arched roof fupported by one pillar, in the centre of the houfe; arched pillars from every angle terminate in the grand pillar. This pillar, nine feet in circumference, is crufted over with fixteen round pilafters or fmall pillars, alternately round and fluted, and twenty-four feet high, adorned with a chapiter, from which arife fixteen round pillars, that fpread along the roof, and join at the top; with the pillars (five in number) rifing from every fide of the octolateral figure. There is a large window in every fide of feven, and the eighth fide communicates with the choir. In the North wall of this Chapter Houfe there are five ftalls, cut by way of niches, for the Bifhop (or the Dean in the Bifhop's abfence) and the dignified clergy to fit in. The middle ftall, for the Bifhop or Dean, is larger, and raifed a ftep higher, than the other four: they were all lined with wainfcot.

Some of the dimenfions of the church may be feen as follows:

	Feet.
The length on the outfide	264
The breadth on the outfide	35
The breadth within the walls	28
The length of the traverfe outfide	114
The length within walls	110
The height of the Weft tower, not including the fpire	84
The height of the tower in the centre, including the fpire	198
The height of the Eaftern turrets	60
The breadth of the great gate	24
The height thereof	24
The breadth of each valve	5
The height of each valve near	10
The height of the fide walls	36
The height of the Chapter Houfe	34
The diagonal breadth within walls	37
The breadth of every fide near	15
The circumference of the great pillar	9
The height thereof below the chapiter	24
The breadth of the porticoes on the fide	18

The

		Feet.
The breadth of the West window	— — —	19
The height thereof	— — —	27
The height of the East windows	— — —	10
The height of the second row	— — —	7
The diameter of the circular window	— — —	10

In taking these dimensions I have not studied a scrupulous exactness, and in some of them it is not possible to do so. The spires of the two West towers are fallen; but the stone work is pretty entire. No part of the great tower, in the middle, now stands. The two Eastern turrets, being winding stair-cases, and vaulted at top, are entire. The walls of the choir are pretty entire; and so is the whole Chapter House; but the walls of the nave and traverse are mostly fallen.

It is a mistake, that this stately edifice was either burnt or demolished by the mob at the Reformation. The following act of Privy Council shews the contrary, viz. " Edinburgh, 14th February, 1567-8. Seeing provision must be made for entertaining the men of war (soldiers) whose service cannot be spared, until the rebellious and disobedient subjects be reduced; therefore appoint, that the lead be taken from the Cathedral Churches in Aberdeen and Elgin, and sold for sustentation of the said men of war. And command and charge the Earl of Huntley, Sheriff of Aberdeen, and his deputes; Alexander Dunbar, of Cumnock, Knight, Sheriff of Elgin and Forres, and his deputes; William, Bishop of Aberdeen; Patrick, Bishop of Moray, &c. That they defend and assist Alexander Clerk and William Bernie, and their servants, in taking down and selling the said lead, &c. Signed R. M." *(Keith's Hist.)*

The lead was accordingly taken off the churches, and shipped at Aberdeen, for Holland; but soon after the ship had left the river, it sunk, which was owing, as many thought, to the superstition of the Roman Catholic Captain. Be this as it may, the Cathedral of Moray being uncovered, was suffered to decay, as a piece of Romish vanity, too expensive to be kept in repair. Some painted rooms in the towers and choir remained so entire about the year 1640, that Roman Catholics repaired to them, there to say their prayers. *(Rec. Presbytery of Elgin.)*

Elgin.) The great tower, in the middle of the church, being uncovered, the wooden work gradually decayed, and the foundation failing, the tower fell, anno 1711, on a Peace Sunday, in the morning: feveral children were playing, and idle people walking within the area of the church, and immediately as they removed to breakfaft, the tower fell down, and no one was hurt.

THE College, when at Spynie, confifted of a Dean, Chancellor, Archdeacon, Chanter, Treafurer, and eight Canons, inftituted by Bifhop Bricius: on the tranflation the Canons were increafed to twenty-two.

THE precinct here was walled round with a ftrong ftone wall, four yards high, and nine hundred in circuit. It had four gates; the Eaft gate, called the Water-gate, or the Pan's Port, appears to have had an iron door, a portcullis, and a porter's lodge; probably the other gates, now fallen, had the fame fences. Within this area ftood the Cathedral and the Canons Houfes.

ON July 3d, 1402, Alexander Mac Donald, third fon of the Lord of the Ifles, entered the College of Elgin, wholly fpoiled and plundered it, and burnt great part of the town; for this he and his officers were excommunicated; but afterwards abfolved, on paying a fum of money, applied to the erection of a crofs and bell, on that part of the chanonry neareft the bridge of Elgin.

THE revenues of this bifhoprick, according to Keith, were: Money 1649l. 7s. 7d. (Scots.) Wheat 10 bolls. Bear 77 c. 6 b. 3 f. 2 p. Oats 2 c. 8 b. Salmon 8 laft c. Poultry n. 223. This plate gives a general view of the Cathedral, as feen on the South Eaft.

CATHEDRAL CHURCH OF ELGIN. PLATE II.

THIS plate fhews the Chapter Houfe of this elegant building. Both views were drawn A. D. 1790.

THE PRIORY OF PLUSCARDEN.

This priory was founded by King Alexander II. in the year 1230. It was dedicated to the honour of St. Andrew, and named Vallis St. Andreæ. It was peopled with Monks of Vallis Caulium, a reform of the Ciftertians, following the rule of St. Bennet. They derived their appellation from the firft priory of that congregation, which was founded by Virard, in the diocefe of Langres, in France, between Dijon and Autun, in Burgundy, in the year 1192. By their conftitutions they were obliged to live an auftere and folitary life. None but the Prior and Procurator were allowed to go without the precinct of the monaftery, for any reafon whatfoever. They were brought into Scotland by William Malvoifin, Bifhop of St. Andrews, in the year 1230, and were fettled at Plufcarden, Beaulieu, and Ardchattan.

These Monks for fome time ftrictly obferved the conftitutions of their order, but at length relaxing in their difcipline, and by degrees becoming vicious, the monaftery was reformed, and from an independent houfe, was degraded to a cell of the Abbey of Dumfermling.

By the munificence of diverfe pious perfons, Kings, and great men, this monaftery became very rich. The whole valley of Plufcarden, three miles in length, in the parifh of Elgin; the lands of Old Milns, near the town of Elgin; fome lands in Durris; and the lands of Grange Hill, belonged to it; at this laft named place, i. e. Grange Hill, the priory had a grange and a cell of Monks. The mills at Old Mills, near Elgin, alfo belonged to this priory. The town lands were thirled to thofe mills, and all grain growing there, or brought in, was to be ground at thofe mills. King Robert Bruce alfo gave the priory a fifhing on the river Spey.

The revenue of this priory, as given in A. D. 1563, was as follows: 525 l. 10s. 1½d. Wheat 1 chalder, 1 boll, 2 firlots. Malt, meal and bear 51 chalders, 4 bolls, 3 firlots, 1 peck. Oats 5 chalders, 13 bolls. Dry multures 9 chalders, 11 bolls. Salmon 30 lafts. Graffums, cain, cuftoms, poultrie, &c. omitted. Deducted anno 1563. To ilk ane of

five

five Monks, in kething and habite silver 16l. And to ilk ane in victual 1 chalder, 5 bolls per annum.

This priory stands on the North side of the river Lochty, about six miles South West from the town of Elgin, near the entry of the valley, at the foot of the North hill, which reverberating the sun beams, renders the place very warm. The walls of the precinct are almost entire, and make nearly a square figure. The church stands about the middle of the square; a fine edifice, in the form of a cross, with a square tower in the middle, all of hewn stone. The Oratory and Refectory join to the South end of the church, under which is the Dormitory.

The Chapter House is a piece of curious workmanship; Shaw* calls it an octagonal cube (by which, I suppose, he means that its height is equal to its diameter). The vaulted roof of this building is supported by one pillar. The lodgings of the Prior, and cells of the Monks were all contiguous to the church. Here are, in different parts, paintings in fresco, on the walls.

Within the precincts were gardens and green walks. In a word, the remains of this priory shew that these Monks lived in a stately palace, and not in mean cottages.

The Prior was Lord of Regality within the priory lands, and had a distinct Regality, in Grange Hill, called "the Regality of Staneforenoon." At the Reformation Sir Alexander Seaton, afterwards Earl of Dunfermline, was, anno 1565, made Commendator of Pluscardon; he disposed of the church lands and the patronage, the lands of Grange Hill, and the Barony of Pluscarden, and Old Mill, 23d February, 1595, to Kenneth Mackenzie, of Kintail, who got a new grant of that barony, dated 12th March, 1607, with all and sundry the teind sheaves of the whole lands and Barony, with their pertinents, which were never separated from the stock, and of which the Prior, and Convent, and their predecessors, were in possession in all times past.

---

* In his History of the Province of Moray.

May 9th, 1633, George, of Kintail, brother and heir of the said Kenneth, difpofed of the Barony to his brother, Thomas Mackenzie; from whom Sir George Mackenzie, of Tarbet, evicted it by a charter of apprifing, anno 1649; and difpofed of it, anno 1662, to the Earl of Caithnefs and Major George Bateman. The Earl transferred his right to the Major, anno 1664; and the Major fold the whole Barony to Ludowick Grant, anno 1677. Here let it be remarked, that Alexander Brodie, of Lethen, father-in-law to Grant, paid the purchafe money, five thoufand pounds fterling; and Grant poffeffed Plufcarden only as a Tutor or Truftee, for his fecond fon, James; and in 1709 refigned it in his favour. From the faid James Grant (the late Sir James) William Duff, of Dipple, purchafed it, anno 1710: and it is now the property of the Earl of Fife.

It is commonly reported that the famous book of Plufcarden, feen and perufed by George Buchanan, was written here; but that book is by many, with great probability, fuppofed to have been only a copy of Fordun, belonging to this monaftery. This view was drawn A. D. 1790.

THE BISHOP'S PALACE AT SPYNIE. PLATE I.

This was the chief palace of the Bifhops of Moray. It ftands on a rifing ground, on the South bank of the Loch of Spynie. This loch was formerly three miles in length; but now, by drains and banks, is much confined.

This edifice, when entire, is faid to have been one of the moft magnificent epifcopal palaces in Scotland. According to Shaw, in his Hiftory of Moray, the buildings occupied an area of fixty yards. In the South Weft corner ftood a ftrong tower, called Davy's Tower, twenty yards long, thirteen broad, and about twenty high: it confifted of vaulted rooms on the ground ftory; and above thefe four apartments of rooms of ftate, and bed rooms, with vaulted clofets or cabinets in the wall, which is nine feet thick, with a flight of broad and eafy ftairs, winding to the top; the whole tower is vaulted at the top; over which is a cape houfe, with a battlement round it. This tower was

built

built by Bishop David Stewart, who died A. D. 1475. This Bishop having some dispute with the Earl of Huntley, laid him under an ecclesiastic censure, at which the Gordons were so much provoked, that they threatened to pull the Bishop out of his pigeon holes, meaning the little old rooms of the former episcopal residence; the Bishop is said to have replied, that he should soon build a house, out of which the Earl and his whole Clan should not be able to pull him.

In the other three corners stood small towers, with narrow rooms. On the south side of the area, between the towers, was a spacious tennis court; and parrallel to it on the inside, a chapel: on the East side, between the turrets, were placed the offices and stables; and the North side was occupied by lodging rooms, store houses, and cellars. The gate or chief entry was in the centre of the East wall, secured by an iron portcullis. Over this gate are placed the arms of Bishop John Innes, with the initials of his name; he was consecrated A. D. 1406: his arms are three stars. This has occasioned a conjecture, though not supported by any other authority, that he was the first who built any part of that court.

In the South wall of David's Tower are placed the arms of Bishops David Stewart and Patrick Heyburn. The precinct of this palace was well fenced with a high and strong wall, and within it were gardens, plots of grass, and pleasant green walks.

In 1590 Sir Alexander Lindsay, son of the Earl of Crawford, was created Lord Spynie, whose grandson dying 1760, without issue, the lands reverted to the crown, and were granted to Douglas, of Spynie; from whom the Barony was purchased by James Brodie, late of Whitehill; and is now the property of James Brodie, his grandson. But the castle and precinct (paying annually about twelve pounds sterling) belong to the crown.

SPYNIE CASTLE. Plate II.

This plate gives a different view of this venerable ruin. Both were drawn A. D. 1790.

FIFESHIRE.

PRIORY OF PITTENWEEM.

PITTENWEEM, in the shire of Fife, was a house of Canons regular of St. Augustine, dedicated to the Virgin Mary, and a cell to the Mitred Priory of St. Andrew's. It was situated in the town of Pittenweem, near the South East corner of the county of Fife; when or by whom it was founded is not mentioned by any writers I have seen. It had a great many lands belonging to it, with the churches of Rind, Anstruther-Wester, &c. which are now erected into a regality, called the regality of Pittenweem, of which the Lairds of Anstruther are heritable Bailies.

COLONEL STUART, Captain of his Majesty's Guards, was appointed Commendator of Pittenweem, in the year 1567. His son, Frederick Stuart, was, in the year 1609, by the favour of King James VI. raised to the dignity of Lord Pittenweem; but dying without male issue, the honour became extinct.

FROM the following story, the original foundation of this monastery took place at a very early period. " St. Fillan, (if we may believe Camerarius, who tells us the story from the Chronicle of Paisley) was born in the shire of Fife, in the seventh century; his father, Feriath, was a nobleman, and his mother's name was Kentigerna. At his birth he appeared like a monster, having something in his mouth like a stone; upon which his father ordered him privately to be drowned, in an adjacent loch; but the boy being preserved by the administration of angels, a holy Bishop, called Ibarus, coming accidentally by, took up the child, and having baptized him, caused bring him up in all virtue and literature, in the monastery of Pittenweem, and at length, upon

the

PITTLESSIE ABBEY.

the death of the Abbot, he was chosen in his place; but some time before his death he retired to the solitary desert of Tyrus, where he spent the remainder of his days in devotion, and died about the year of our Lord 649."*

ANNO 1527 John, Prior of Pittenweem, was a subscriber to the sentence pronounced against the Abbot of Ferm, declaring him an Heretic.

THE account of the profits given in at the Reformation, amounted in money to the sum of 412l. 12s. 6d.; 4 chaldron and 5 bolls of wheat; 7 chaldron and 2 bolls of bear; 4 chaldron, 12 bolls, 2 firlots, 1½ peck of meal; 7 chaldron, 2 bolls, 1 firlot, 3½ pecks of oats; 1 chaldron and 11 bolls of peas; and 20 chaldron of salt.

THIS view was drawn A. D. 1784.

ROSEYTHE CASTLE.

THIS castle stands in the county of Fife, a little above the North Ferry, opposite Hopetoun House. I have not been able to learn at what time, or by whom, it was built. Sir Robert Sibbald describes it in his History of Fife. " The Castle of Roseythe," says he, " is remarkable, being situated upon a rock that advances a little into the Forth: the water at full tide surrounds it, and makes it an island. It was anciently the seat of the Stuarts, of Roseythe, or Dunideer, brother Germain to Walter the great Stuart of Scotland, father to King Robert II.; that family failed lately: the last Laird of that name dying unmarried, without brother or children, disposed the estate to a stranger; and it is at present the possession of Primrose, Earl of Roseberry."

THE tradition of the country, however unfounded, is, that the mother of Oliver Cromwell was born in this castle, and that the protector himself therefore visited it during the time he commanded the army in Scotland. It is at present the property of Lord Hopetoun.

---

* M'Kenzie's Lives of the Sco.Writ. 1. 272, 273.

On the Weft fide of the door, on the South wall of this caftle, is the following infcription:

IN DEV TYM DRAV YIS CORD YE BEL TO CLINC
QVHAIS MERY VOCE VARNIS TO MEAT & DRINC.

In one of the barns belonging to Mr. Walker, at Orchard Head, is a ftone, which he picked out of the rubbifh of this caftle; on it is this infcription:

GOD GRANT AL GLOIR
I MAY ESCHEV
BOT IN THE CROS
OF CHRIST IESV.

This view was drawn A. D. 1784.

THE ABBEY OF BALMERINO.

This was a Ciftertian Abbey, of which Keith gives the following account: " Balmerino, or Balmerinach, in Fifefhire, called by Lefly Balmuræum, and by Fordun Habitaculum ad Mare, was an abbey of a beautiful ftructure; begun by King Alexander II. and his mother, Emergarda, daughter to the Earl of Beaumont, in the year 1229. This lady bought the lands of Balmarinach, and paid therefore a thoufand marks fterling, to Richard de Ruele, fon of Henry, who refigned Balmerinach, Cultrach, and Balandean, in the court of King Alexander, at Forfar, the day after the feaft of St. Dennis, in the year 1215; upon which ground Emergarda founded this monaftery; which was of old a ftately building, pleafantly fituated near the fhore, hard by the falt water of Tay. It is now for the moft part in ruins. The Monks of this place, which was dedicated to St. Edward, as well as the Virgin Mary, were brought from Melrofs. David de Lindfay gave them an annuity out of his mill of Kirkbuit, which was confirmed by King Alexander II. in the year 1233.

Symon, fon and heir of Symon de Kennir, granted them, in perpetual alms, a moiety of all his lands, in the feud of Kinnir, which is now called

called little Kennir; his charter was confirmed by the faid King Alexander, 21ft September, and the 22d of his reign. The Preceptory of Gadvan, near Denbug, in Fife, with the houfe and lands, belonged alfo to this abbey, and two or three Monks of their order conftantly refided in that place.

LAURENCE DE ABERNETHIE, fon of Orm, gave to this monaftery, Corbie, called alfo Birkhill, from a park of birch trees, furrounding the houfe; the reafon for this donation is expreffed in this charter, which was, becaufe Queen Emergarda, who died 3d Id. of February, anno 1233, had by her teftament left him two hundred marks fterling; fhe being buried before the high altar, in the Church of Balmerinach; he, out of refpect to her memory and the place of her fepulture, gave this benefaction.

AFTER the Reformation King James VI. erected Balmerinach into a temporal lordfhip, in favour of James Elphinftone, of Barnton, Principal Secretary of State, the 20th April, 1604; he had likewife been a Lord of Seffion, and Prefident after the Lord Fivie.

THE revenues of this abbey, as given in anno 1562: Money 704l. 2s. 10½d. (Scots). Wheat 4 c. Bear 21 c. 12 b. 3 f. 3½ p. Oats 4 c. 14 b. 1 f. 3½ p.; to which the Affumption Book adds: Meal 15 c. 12 b. 2 f.; and poultry n. 763.

DUMFERMLING ABBEY. PLATE I.

DUMFERMLING was a Benedictine Monaftery, in the fhire of Fife, fituated about four miles above Queen's Ferry. It was begun by King Malcolm III. or Canmore, and was finifhed by King Alexander I. furnamed the Fierce. It was famous for being the burial place of feveral of the Kings of Scotland. It is by fome thought to have been originally intended for an hofpital or infirmary, being ftyled in fome old manufcripts, Monafterium ab Monte Infirmorum. At firft it was governed by a Prior; but David I. changed it into an abbey, and brought into it, in the year 1124, thirteen Monks, from Canterbury: but at the Diffolution there were twenty-fix.

Its endowments were very confiderable; one in particular granted by David I. has caufed much fpeculation; this was " the tyth of all the gold found in Fife and Fotheriff," which has been confidered as a proof that gold was frequently found in the ftreams flowing from the hills."

ANOTHER grant, from the fame Monarch, invefts this monaftery with a right to part of the feals taken at Kinghorn; and a third, by Malcolm IV. gives them the heads (except the tongues) of certain fmall Whales, called Crefpeis, which might be taken in fuch parts of Scotch water (the Firth of Forth) where the church ftood; and the oil extracted from them was to be employed for its ufe.

BOTH King Malcolm and King Alexander beftowed feveral confiderable eftates on thefe Monks; among them Muffelburgh and Inverefk, with the parifh church, mills, and harbour, were given by King Malcolm and his fon, St. David. Burnt Ifland, called of old Wefter-Kinghorn, with its caftle and harbour, belonged alfo to this place, with Kinghorn, Kirkaldy, and feveral other towns, &c. mentioned in the Chartulary of this houfe, in the Advocate's Library.

THE firft Abbot of this monaftery was Gosfridus, of whom the Hiftory of Florence, of Worcefter, gives the following account: " A man of fingular piety, Prior of Canterbury, by name Gosfridus, was, at the requeft of David, King of the Scots, and with the approbation of Archbifhop William, elected Abbot of the place in Scotland, called Dumfermling; but he was ordained by Robert, Bifhop of St. Andrew's, in the year 1128. This Gosfridus died in the year 1153: for the Chronicle of the Holy Crofs, at the aforefaid year, fays, Gosfridus, the firft Abbot of Dumfermling, died, and his nephew, Gaufridus, fucceeded in his place. The laft Abbot was George Durie, Commendator and Archdeacon of St. Andrew's. The church and monaftery were dedicated to the Holy Trinity, and St. Margaret, Queen of Scotland; it was united to the crown by the 189th act of King James VIth's 13th parliament.

AT the General Diffolution of the Monafteries, Dumfermling was firft given to Secretary Pitcairn, then to the mafter of Gray, and afterwards was conferred upon Alexander Seton, a younger fon of George Lord Seton, who was at firft advanced to the honour of a Peer of the Realm,

Realm, by the title of Lord Urquhart, the 3d Auguft, 1591; and on the 3d of March, 1605, was created Earl of Dumfermling. This title became extinct in 1694 for want of iffue. Muffelburgh was likewife erected into a lordfhip, in favour of the Lord Thirlefton, and excepted from the general annexation made in the year 1587: and by the fame act the conventual brethren of this place, having embraced the Reformation, were no ways to be deprived of their portions during their life time.

The remains of this abbey are very extenfive, and alfo fhew it was once an elegant building. The Fratery, with its beautiful window, is extremely ftriking. The Abbot's houfe is adjacent. In 1303 Edward I. burned down the whole abbey, except the church and cells: his excufe for this facrilegious barbarity was, that it gave a retreat to his enemies.

Part of the church is now ufed for parochial fervice. it is supported by maffy pillars, fcarcely feventeen feet high, and thirteen and a half in circumference; two are ribbed fpirally, and marked with zig-zag lines, refembling thofe of Durham: this is accounted for from its having been built by Malcolm Canmore, at the inftance of Turgot, Bifhop of St. Andrew's, who had been Prior of Durham. The arches of this part are femicircular. The infide, like thofe of moft of the Scotch churches, is very ill kept, and ftrangely lumbered up with pews. The South fide feems as if it had been like to give way, being fupported by a number of clumfy buttreffes, apparently more modern than the reft of the building.

In this church is the tomb of Robert Pitcairn, Commendator of this Abbey, and Secretary of State, in the beginning of the reign of James VI. in the Regency of Lenox. He died in the Caftle of Loch Levin in 1584. Notwithftanding the praifes beftowed on him in his epitaph, tradition fays, he did not efcape the tongue of detraction, to which the following infcription, cut over the door of his houfe, in the Maygate, is faid to allude :

SEN VORD IS THRALL AND THOCHT IS FRE
KEIP VEILL THY TONGE I COINSELL THE.

Tradition fays he was accufed of incontinence.

Here.

HERE, as has been before observed, several of the Kings of Scotland were buried; these were Malcolm, Edgar, Alexander, David I. Malcolm IV. Alexander II. and Robert Bruce; the two first apart, the others under as many flat stones, each nine feet long. The Queen of Malcolm is also here interred. Here is likewise the tomb of Robert Pitcairn, the Commendator above-mentioned.

KING MALCOLM CANMORE had a castle here; some small remains of it, situated on a mount, in Mr. Phyn's gardens, at Pittencrief, are still visible; and ther is a popular story of a subterraneous passage from it to the monastery. A palace was afterwards built on the side next the town, which falling to decay, was rebuilt by Anne of Denmark, as appears by the following inscription:

Propylæum et superstructas ædes vetustate et injuriis temporum collapsas dirutasque; a fundamentis in hanc ampliorem formam restituit et instauravit ANNA Regina FREDERICA DANORUM Regis Augustissimi Filia: anno salutis 1600.

THIS palace is now quite in ruins; but nevertheless it may be plainly seen. It was once a magnificent building. Here was born that unfortunate monarch King Charles I. A gateway intervenes between the royal residence and the Abbey Church.

THIS view shews the North side of the church and palace, called the King's House, drawn from a chamber window in the New Inn.

DUMFERMLING ABBEY. PLATE II.

THIS plate gives a general view of these magnificent ruins. The building opposite, on the left, is the Fratery; to the right of it is the church and the scattered arches and window; on the right of all is said to be the burial-place of some of the Kings.

THE FRATERY OF DUMFERMLING ABBEY.

THIS view shews the beautiful window of the Fratery or Refectory, viewed on the outside, and its adjoining gate. It was, with the other views of this abbey, drawn A. D. 1790.

THE

DUNFERMLINE ABBEY Pl.2

ST. ANDREW'S (UPPER FIELD,) BERKELEY.

THE CATHEDRAL OF ST. ANDREW'S.

This was the metropolitical church of Scotland, removed hither by Ungus, in 518, after the conquest of the Picts. This was the Prince who first made the cross of St. Andrew the Scottish badge.

In the year 1441 St. Andrew's was erected into an Archbishoprick, by Pope Sixtus IV. at the intercession of James III.

The Cathedral was begun by Bishop Arnold, anno 1161; he dying the same year, the work seems to have proceeded very slowly, since it was not completed by Bishop Lamberton till the year 1318, one hundred and fifty-seven years from the time it was first begun.

The following measures shew it was a very large building, and the remains evince it was elegantly finished. Its figure was that of a cross; its length from East to West measured three hundred and seventy feet; the transept three hundred and twenty-two.

Of this magnificent building nothing remains above ground but fragments of the East and West ends; the South wall of the choir, measuring in length about one hundred and eighty feet, and thirty in height: there is also a wall at right angles to the choir, possibly part of the South transept; the rest was destroyed by Knox and his sacrilegious followers.

The West end consists of a large gate, with a pointed arch, called the Golden Gate, probably from its having been once gilt; over it are a series of arches, above which was a large window: on each side of the gate was a polygonal tower, crowned with a conical top. That on the North side is fallen down.

The East end has also two turrets, crowned with pointed tops, between which were three windows, and over it a large one, nearly occupying the whole interval between the turrets.

In the South wall is a range of windows with pointed arches; but in part supposed to have been the South transept: the windows are circular, and at the bottom there runs a range of interlaced semicircular arches.

At the East end is the chapel of St. Regulus, chiefly remarkable for its tower, which is a square of twenty feet; its height an hundred and three, or, as some have it, an hundred and six, feet.

The body of this chapel is still remaining; but the two side aisles are demolished. The doors and windows are round; some of their arches contain more than a semicircle. It has lately been repaired at the public expence.

THE DOMINICANS, OR BLACK FRIARS, ST. ANDREW'S.

This is said to be part of the Convent of Black Friars, probably the chapel; it stands on the right hand side of the main street, going towards the Cathedral, and seems, though small, to have been a handsome building. Its arched stone roof greatly resembles that of the College of Lincluden, near Dumfries. Here are neither monuments nor inscriptions.

The Grammar School is within its precincts, and by some supposed to have been a part of the original building; but now entirely modernised.

The Dominicans or Black Friars, of St. Andrew's, Keith says, were founded by William Wishart, Bishop of that city, in the year 1274, and placed at the West part of the street, called the Northgate. King James V. annexed to this house, at St. Andrew's, the Convents of Coupar and St. Monan's, both in Fife, at the desire of Friar John Adamson, Professor of Divinity, and Provincial of the Order in Scotland. The charter is dated at Edinburgh, the 23d January, the eighth year of his reign. This view was drawn A. D. 1790.

THE CASTLE OF ST. ANDREW'S.

This castle stands by the sea side, on a ridge of rocks North of the town, said to have been accessible only by a narrow passage. On the East and North the ruins of the walls, and the perpendicular rock

below,

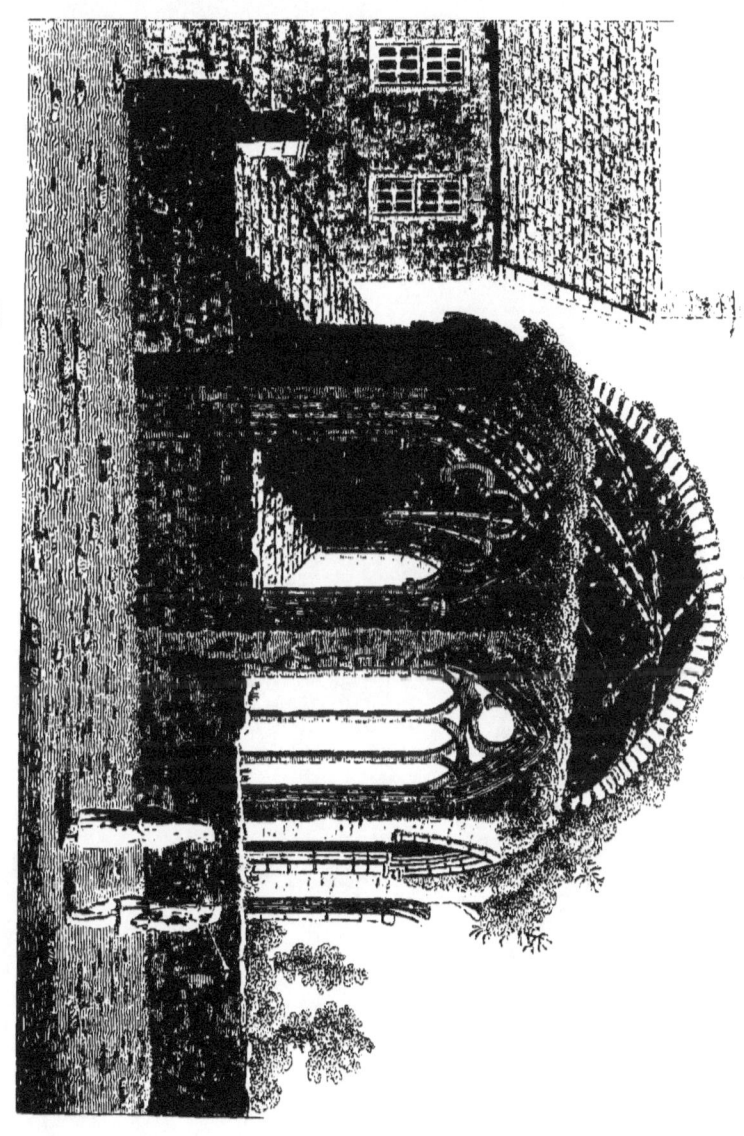

THE CHAPEL OF THE BLACKFRIARS

CASTLE of ST ANDREWS.

below, are a great height above the sea, which at high water, beats againſt them. The South wall has fallen to the water's edge; large fragments of the South Eaſt wall have tumbled inwards, and formed a ſteep bank, covered with graſs and weeds, not eaſily paſſable. The great ſquare tower is ſtill ſufficiently entire to give ſome idea of the elegance of the building.

This caſtle was built in the year 1155, by Roger, Biſhop of this ſee: he died in 1202. It appears that at this time the ſea did not approach to its walls, for a little to the South Eaſt are ſtill to be ſeen, at low water, the remains of a ſmall chapel. Beſides this we alſo learn from ſome old writings, of an eſtate in the neighbourhood, that the proprietor had the privilege of driving his cattle and goods on the Eaſt ſide of the caſtle, which for ſome centuries paſt no man could have done.

CARDINAL BEATON greatly repaired and beautified this building. From a window in it he is ſaid to have enjoyed the cruel ſpectacle of Wiſhart's execution, who was burnt for hereſy on a ſmall green oppoſite the caſtle.

IN the year 1546 Norman Leſlie, brother to the Earl of Rothes, with ſome of his followers, ſeizing the porter by ſurpriſe, made themſelves maſter of the caſtle, when one of them, Peter Carmichael, ran immediately to the Cardinal's chamber, and ſlew him, and afterwards expoſed his body out of the very window whence he had ſeen the death of Wiſhart.

THE perſons concerned in this murder ſeized and held out the caſtle for a year, though beſieged by the French commander with two great cannon, called Crook-mow and Deaf-meg.

THEY afterwards ſurrendered to a French fleet, in July 1547, and were tranſported to France. The caſtle was in purſuance of an act of council, demoliſhed, leſt it ſhould ſerve as a receptacle for rebels; and perhaps leſt it ſhould be occupied by the Engliſh, who were then expected to invade Scotland.

THERE is a common tradition, that this caſtle was demoliſhed by Cromwell. This ſeems to be groundleſs; if that was the caſe, it muſt have previouſly been rebuilt or repaired. This view was drawn in 1790.

DEN

DEN MILN CASTLE.

THE following account of this caftle is taken from Sir Robert Sibbald's Hiftory of Fife:

"DEN MILN CASTLE was antiently the Earl of Fyfe's; and after the forefaulture King James II. anno reg. 14, gave it to his beloved and familiar fervant James Balfour, fon to Sir John Balfour, of Balgarvie, Knight; and is now the feat of Sir Michael Balfour, his lineal fucceffor. Sir James Balfour; Lord Lyon, a moft knowing antiquary; and Sir Andrew Balfour, a very learned phyfician, were fons of this houfe, and brothers; vide Memor Belfourian. Hard by it is Clatchart-Craig, an high rock; on the top of it was antiently a ftrong caftle." This view was drawn A. D. 1790.

ARGYLESHIRE.

DUNSTAFFAGE CASTLE LORNE.

THE builder of this caftle and time of its conftruction are unknown; it is certainly of great antiquity, and was once the feat of the Pictifh and Scottifh Princes. Here for a long time was preferved the famous ftone, the Palladium of Scotland, brought, as the legend has it, from Spain. It was afterwards removed by Kenneth II. to Scone, and is now in Weftminfter Abbey; brought hither by King Edward I. On it was the following infcription:

> Ni fallat fatum Scoti quocunque locatum
> Invenient lepidem, regnare tenantur ibidem.

THE caftle is fquare; the infide only eighty-feven feet: it is partly in ruins, though in other parts habitable. Three of the angles have round towers, one of them projecting but very little. The entrance is towards the fea, at prefent by a ftair-cafe; but, probably, in former times, by a draw-bridge, which fell from a fmall gateway; the mafonry appears very ancient; the tops embattled or crenellated. This building is fituated on a rock, whofe fides have been fcarped down to the form of the caftle, in order to render it fteep and difficult of accefs.

In 1307 this caftle was held by Alexander Mac Dougal, Lord of Argyle, a friend to the Englifh; but it was that year taken by Robert Bruce, when Mac Dougal fuing to that Prince for peace, was received into his favour.

ABOUT the year 1455 this caftle appears to have been the refidence of the Lords of the Ifles; for here James, laft Earl of Douglas, after his defeat in Annandale, fled to Donald, the Regulus of the time, and prevailed on him to take arms, and carrying on a plundering war againft his Monarch, James II.

At a small distance from the castle is a ruined chapel, once an elegant building, and at one end an enclosure, serving for a family cemetery. Near this place is a very remarkable echo.

According to vulgar tradition this castle was founded by Edwin, a Pictish Monarch, cotemporary with Julius Cæsar, who named it after himself, Evonium. Dun Staffage signifies Stephen's Mount.

This view was drawn A. D. 1772.

NEWARK CASTLE. Renfrewshire.

This was the castle or principal mansion of the barony of Finlaystun Maxwell, which, about the middle of the fifteenth century, with diverse other lands, came to Sir Robert Maxwell, of Calderwood, a younger son of the family of Nether Pollock, in right of Elizabeth, his wife, second daughter and co-heiress of Sir Robert Dennieſtoun, of that ilk. It continued in the possession of the Maxwell family for several generations, till sold by George Maxwell, alias Napier, of Kilmahew, Esq; to Mr. William Cockrane, of Kilmaronock, about the beginning of the eighteenth century. It is at present the property of —— Hamilton, of Wishaw, Esq; in whose family it has been for a considerable length of time.

This castle stands on the Eastern point of the bay, which contains the town and harbour of Port Glasgow and Newark. It is now in ruins; but some part of it was inhabited about fifty years ago. It consists of a square court, with high walls, round turrets, and battlements. Over the main door are the arms of Maxwell, very much defaced, having beneath them this inscription: " The blessing of God be herein, anno 1597." On another part of one of the North windows is engraved the date 1599. Over most of the windows are the letters P. M. being the initials of Sir Patrick Maxwell, who probably built the modern part of it. The tower is of more ancient date than the rest; when or by whom it was built is not known.

This view was drawn A. D. 1772.

ISLE

ISLE OF ARRAN.

BRODIE CASTLE.

THE following account of this caftle is given by Mr. Pennant; " Brodie Caftle feated on an eminence amidft flourifhing plantations, above a fmall bay open to the Eaft. This place has not at prefent much the appearance of a fortrefs, having been modernifed; it is inhabited by the Duke of Hamilton's Agent, who entertained me with the utmoft civility. It is a place of much antiquity, and feems to have been the fort held by the Englifh, under Sir John Haftings, in 1306, when it was furprifed by the partizans of Robert Bruce, and the garrifon put to the fword. It was demolifhed in 1456 by the Earl of Rofs, in the reign of James II. It is faid to have been rebuilt by James V. and to have been garrifoned in the time of Cromwell's ufurpation. Few are the records of thefe diftant places, therefore very wide muft be their hiftoric gaps."

RANZA CASTLE.

THIS caftle ftands on a low projecting neck of land, and guards the entrance into a fmall harbour.

IT was founded by one of the Scottifh Monarchs; and is of fome antiquity, for Fordun, who wrote about the year 1380, fpeaks of this and Borthwick as royal caftles.

THIS building confifts of two fquare towers united. It is built with a red grit ftone. In one room is a chimney-piece and fire-place large enough to have roafted an entire ox. It is now abandoned and in ruins.

THIS view was drawn A. D. 1772.

ISLE OF SKY.

DUNVEGAN CASTLE.

THE Caſtle of Dunvegan ſtands on a high rock, over a loch of the ſame name, a branch of Loch Falart; part of it has been repaired in the modern taſte, but the greater portion of it is ancient. The oldeſt part is a ſquare tower, which, with a wall round the edge of the rock, was the original fortification.

" In this caſtle," ſays Mr. Pennant, " is preſerved the Braolauch-ſhi, or fairy flag of the family, beſtowed on it by Titania, the Ben Shi, or wife of Oberon, King of the Fairies; ſhe bleſſed it at the ſame time with powers of the firſt importance, which were to be exerted only on three occaſions: but on the laſt, after the end was obtained, an inviſible being is to arrive and carry off the ſtandard and ſtandard bearer, never more to be ſeen. A family of *Clan y Faitter* had this dangerous office, and held it by three lands in Bracadale.

THE flag has been produced thrice, the firſt time in an unequal engagement againſt the *Clan-Ronald*, to whoſe ſight the Macleods were multiplied ten fold; the ſecond preſerved the heir of the family, being then produced to ſave the longings of the lady of the family; and the third time to ſave my own; but it was ſo tattered that Titania did not ſeem to think it worth ſending for.

THIS was a ſuperſtition derived from the Norwegian anceſtry of the houſe, the fable was caught from the country, and might be of uſe to animate the Clan. The Danes had their magical ſtandard *Raefan*, or, the Raven, embroidered in an inſtant by the three daughters of *Lodbroke* and ſiſters of *Hinguar*, *Hubbar* or *Ivar*.* *Sigurd* had an enchanted flag

---

* Aſſer. vit. Alfred 10.

given

ISLE OF SKY.

given him by his mother, with circumſtances ſomewhat ſimilar to the Dunvegan colours; whoſoever wore it in the day of battle was to be killed; accordingly in one of his battles, three ſtandard bearers were ſucceſſively ſlain, but on the death of the laſt he obtained the victory.*

HERE is preſerved a great ox-horn tipped with ſilver; the arm was twiſted round its ſpires, the mouth brought over the elbow, and then drank off. The Northern nations held this ſpecies of cup in high eſteem, and uſed the capacious horns of the great *Aurochs*.† They graced the hoſpitable halls of Kings,‡ and out of them the ancient heroes quenched their thirſt: *Ilaquin*,§ weary with ſlaughter, calls aloud for the mighty draught.

Heu labor immenſus, feſſos quam vellicat Artus!
Quis mihi jam præbet cornua plena mero!

IN this caſtle is alſo preſerved a round ſhield made of iron, that even in its decayed ſtate weighs near twenty pounds; itſelf a load in theſe degenerate days: yet they were in uſe no longer ago than in the beginning of the laſt century. Each Chieftain had his armour bearer, who preceded his maſter in time of war, and by my author's‖ account in time of peace; for they went armed even to church, in the manner the North Americans do at preſent in the frontier ſettlements, and for the ſame reaſon, the dread of ſavages.

IN times long before thoſe the ancient Scotch uſed round targets, made of oak, covered with the hides of bulls, and long ſhields, narrow below, and broad above, formed of pieces of oak or willow, ſecured with iron: I gueſs them to be of the ſame kind with the Norwegian ſhields figured by Wormius,¶ and probably derived from the ſame

---

* Torfæus 27.
† *Urorum* Cornibus, Barbari ſeptentrionales potant, urnaſque binas capitis unius cornua implent. Plinii lib. II. c. 37.
‡ Saxo Grammat. 94.
§ Wormii Mon. Dan. 389.
‖ Timothy Poat's MS. Advoc. Library.
¶ Vide fig. 1. tab. XX.

country; they had also a guard for their shoulders, called Scapul;*
and for offensive weapons had the bow, sword, two-handed sword, and
Lochaber ax, a weapon likewise of Norwegian origin; but the image-
tombs of ancient warriors are the best lectures on this subject." To the
list of offensive weapons used by the Scotch, may be added, leaden
mallets † and Jedburgh staves; the latter are described by Major. ‡

---

* Vide fig. 1. tab. XX.
† Lamb's Battle of Flodden.
‡ Hist. Major Britt. p. 198.

INCH COLM.

THE ABBEY OF INCH COLM. Plate I.

THIS monastery stands on an island called Æmonia, in the Forth, and commonly denominated Inch Colm; i. e. the island of Columba, situated about six miles West of the island of Inch Keith, and within about a mile and a half of the Queen's Ferry. According to Fordun it owed its foundation to the following occasion:

"About the year 1123 King Alexander the First having some business of state which obliged him to cross over at the Queen's Ferry, was overtaken by a terrible tempest, blowing from the South West; this obliged the sailors to make for this island of Æmonia, which they reached with the greatest risque and difficulty; here they found a poor hermit, who lived a religious life, according to the rules of St. Columba, and performed service in a small chapel, supporting himself by the milk of one cow, and the shell fish he could pick up on the shore; nevertheless, out of these small means, he entertained the King and his retinue for three days, the time which they were confined here by the wind. During the storm, and whilst at sea, and in the greatest danger, the King made a vow, that if Saint Columba would bring him safe to that island, he would there found a monastery to his honor, and which should be an asylum and relief to navigators: he was moreover farther moved to this foundation, by having from his childhood entertained a particular veneration and honour for that Saint, derived from his parents, who were long married without issue, until imploring the aid of St. Columba, their request was most graciously granted.

This monastery was founded for Canons regular of St. Augustine, and dedicated to the honor of St. Columba. King Alexander endowed it with many benefactions. Alan de Mortimer, Knight, Lord of Aberdour,

dour, gave alfo to God and the Monks of this Abbey, the entire moiety of the lands of his town of Aberdour, for a burying place of himfelf and pofterity, in the church of that monaftery.

WALTER BOWMAKER, Abbot of this place, was one of the continuators of John Fordun's Scoti-Chronicon, as is to be feen in the Liber Carthufianorum de Perth, in the Advocate's Library. He died in the year 1449. James Stewart, of Bieth, a Cadet of the Lord Ocheltree, was made Commendator of Inch Colm on the furrender of Henry, Abbot of that monaftery. In the year 1543 his fecond fon, Henry Stewart, was, by the fpecial favour of King James VI. created a Peer, by the title of Lord St. Colm, in the year 1611.

In Keith's Appendix, refpecting this abbey, he fays: " S. Mone 4261.* There is nothing elfe concerning this rental except in A.† and even there it is very confufed, though given up by James Stewart, who moft probably has been Abbot himfelf. The beft I could make of it is thus: Wheat 2 c. 8 b. 1 f. 10 b. Bear 8 c. 9 b. Meal 14 c. 14 b. Oats 11 c. 12 b."

FORDUN records feveral miracles done by St. Columba, as punifhments to the Englifh, who often pillaged this monaftery. The firft was in the year 1335, when the Englifh ravaging the coaft along the Forth, one veffel, larger than the reft, entered this ifland, and the crew landing, plundered the monaftery of all their moveables, as well worldly as ecclefiaftical; among diverfe ftatues and images carried off, was a famous one of St. Columba, which was kept in the church. It feems as if that Saint did not relifh the voyage, for he raifed fuch a ftorm that it threatened immediate deftruction to the facrilegious veffel, by driving it on the rocks of Inch Keith. The failors, on their near approach to thefe rocks, were terribly alarmed, cried peccavi, afked pardon of the Saint, promifed reftitution of their plunder, and a handfome prefent into the bargain. On this the veffel got fafely into port in that ifland, where, as if raifed from the dead, they landed with great re-

---

* S. the Affignation and Surplus Books.
† A. the Books of Affumption.

joicings;

joicings; they then difembarked the Saint and their other plunder, and tranfported them, with an handfome oblation of gold and filver, to certain inhabitants of Kinghorn, whom they likewife fent payment for their labour, with directions that the whole fhould be fafely delivered to the Monks, from whom they were taken. No fooner was this done, than a favourable wind fprung up, by which this veffel reached St. Abb's Head before the reft of the fleet, not without forming a refolution never more to meddle with St. Columba. It neverthelefs appears that this example was forgotten by the next year, for, from the fame authority, we learn, that in the year 1336 fome other Englifh veffels plundered the church of Dolor, belonging to the Abbot of this houfe, and carried away a beautiful carved wainfcot, with which he had adorned the choir; this they had taken down piecemeal, and fhipped fo as it might be put up in any other place. It was put on board a particular barge, the failors of which rejoicing at their plunder, failed away with pipes and trumpets founding; but St. Columba in an inftant turned their mirth into forrow, for the veffel fuddenly funk to the bottom like a ftone or piece of lead, neither plank nor man being ever more feen. The remaining failors of the fleet, terrified at this judgment, vowed in future they would not trefpafs on that Saint, or on any perfon or thing belonging to him. This event gave rife to a proverb in England, the fubftance of which was, That St. Columba was not to be offended with impunity. They likewife gave him the nick name of Saint Quhalme.

NOTWITHSTANDING the refolution here mentioned, in the year 1384 the Englifh fleet being again in the Forth, plundered this monaftery, which they attempted to burn, and actually fet fire to a fhed near the church; and when the deftruction of the whole monaftery feemed inevitable, fome pious perfons addreffing themfelves to their guardian Saint, he fuddenly changed the wind, which blew back the flames. The plunderers returned to their fhips with their booty, and afterwards landed at the Queen's Ferry, and began to pillage the coaft of the cattle, when they were fuddenly attacked by Thomas and Nicholas Erfkine and Alexander de Lindefay, having with them about fifty horfemen from the Eaft, and William Conyngham, of Kilmaures, with

thirty

INCH COLM.

thirty from the West; these engaging the robbers, flew and wounded some, took others prisoners, and drove a number of them to their veſſels: of these above forty, and those some of the forwardest among the incendiaries, for safety, hung to the anchor, when a sailor dreading the attack of the Scots, cut the cable with an ax, whereby all those who hung about the anchor, were drowned. But what was most wonderful was, that the person who had planned this sacrilege, and been the most active in setting fire to the buildings, was taken prisoner by William de Conyngham, and whilst on the way with him, was seized with the most frantic madness, accusing himself of the above offences, testifying that he had been the most active in burning the shed, and that whilst so employed, he saw St. Columba extinguishing the fire, when that saint caused some volatile flames to dart upon him, which destroyed his beard and eye-brows; his fury increasing, he was killed, and buried in a crofs way near the town of Dony-place.

In the Duke of Somerset's expedition, first of Edward VI. this monastery was after the battle of Pinkey or Muſſelborough, occupied as a post commanding the Forth. The circumstance is recorded by Patin, in the following words:

"Tuesday, the 13th of September in the afternoon my Lords Grace rowed up the Fryth, a vi or vii myles Weſtward, as it runneth into the land, and took in his way an iſland thear called Sainct Coomes Ins, which ſtandeth a iiii. mile beyond Lieth, and a good way ner at the North ſhore than the South, yet not within a mile of the nereſt. It is but half a myle about, and hath in it a pretty abbey (but ye monks were gone) freſh water enough, and alſo coonyes; and is ſo naturally ſtrong, as but one way it can be entered. The plot whearof my Lordes Grace confidering, did quickly caſt to have it kept, whearby all traffik of merchaundife, all commodities els comyng by the Fryth into their land, and utterly ye whole uſe of the Fryth itſelf, with all the havens uppon it, ſhould quyte be taken from them.

Saturday, 17th of September, Sir John Luttrell, Knight, havyng bene by my Lords Grace, and the counſell, elect abbot, by God's ſuffraunce, of the monaſtery of Sainct Coomes Ins, afore remembered, in the afternoon of this day departed towardes the iſland to be ſtalled in

his

INCH COLM.

his fee thear accordyngly; and had with him a coovent of a C. hakbutters and L. pioners, to kepe his houfe and land thear, and ii rowe barkes well furnifhed with municion, and lxx mariners, for them to kepe his waters, whereby it is thought he fhall foon becum a prelate of great powr. The perfytnes of his religion is not alwaies to tarry at home, but fumtime to rowe out abrode a vifitacion, and when he goithe, I have hard fay he taketh alweyes his fumners in barke with hym, which are very open mouthed, and never talk but they are harde a mile of, fo that either for loove of his bleffynges, or fear of his curfinges, he is like to be fouveraigne over moft of his neighbours."

GREAT part of this monaftery is ftill remaining; the cloyfters, with rooms over them, enclofing a fquare area, are quite entire; the pit or prifon, is a moft difmal hole, though lighted by a fmall window; the refectory is up one pair of ftairs; in it, near the window, is a kind of feparate clofet, up a few fteps, commanding a view of the monks when at table; this is fuppofed to have been the Abbot's feat; adjoining to the refectory is a room, from the fize of its chimney, probably the kitchen.

THE octagonal Chapter-houfe, with its ftone roof, is alfo ftanding; over it is a room of the fame fhape, in all likelihood, the place where the charters were kept. Here are the remains of an infcription, in the black letter, which began with Stultus. The infide of the whole building feems to have been plaiftered. Near the water there is a range of offices. Near the Chapter-houfe is the remains of a very large femicircular arch.

IN the adjoining grounds lies the old carved ftone, faid to be a Danifh monument, engraved by Sir Robert Sibbald, in whofe book it is delineated as having a human head at each end; at prefent it is fo defaced by time or weather, that nothing like a head can be diftinguifhed at either end: indeed it requires the aid of a creative fancy, to make out any of the fculpture; fomething like a man with a fpear is feen (by fharp-fighted antiquaries) on the North fide; and on the South, the figure of a crofs; this ftone has been moved from its original fituation.

THIS view fhews the range of buildings near the Sea, the entrance into

into the cloyſters, and the Chapter-houſe, with the **tower of the church,** and fragment of the large arch above-mentioned.

THE ABBEY OF INCH COLM. Plate II.

This plate gives a nearer view of the entrance into the cloyſter, the tower of the church and large arch.

THE ABBEY OF INCH COLM. Plate III.

This view preſents the remains of the church, with part of the great arch, as viewed from a different ſtation.

Plates I. and II. were drawn A. D. 1789, and plate III. in 1790.

ADDENDA TO CASTLE CAMPBELL, PERTHSHIRE.

THE name of this caftle was originally the Caftle of Gloom, which was changed by act 39 Parl. James IV. anno 1489: " Our fouvrane Lord of his royal autoritie, at the defyre and fupplicatioun of his coufing and traift counfallour Colone Erle of Argyle, lord Campbell, and of Lorne his chancellor, hes changeit the name of the caftell and place quhik was callit the Glume, perteining to his faid coufing, and in this parliament makis mutation and changeing of the faid name, and ordanis the famin caftell to be callit in tyme to cum Campbell."—*Black Acts*, p. 89.

THE ABBEY OF CAMBUSKENNETH, STIRLINGSHIRE.

THE Abbey of Cambufkenneth is, in fact, fituated in the fhire of Clackmannan; yet, on account of its large poffeffions in Stirlingfhire, was commonly deemed of that county: it ftood on the border thereof, and its Abbots were frequently denominated abbots of Striveling.

THIS abbey, once the richeft in Scotland, ftands half a mile N. E. of the town of Stirling, upon the north bank of the Forth, and in a fort of peninfula formed by that winding river. The adjacent fields had been the fcene of fome tranfaction, in which one of the Scottifh monarchs, who bore the name of Kenneth, had been concerned, and from thence the place received the name of Cambufkenneth, which fignified the field or creek of Kenneth.

THE monaftery was founded by David I. in the year 1147, and filled with canons regular of the order of St. Auguftine, brought from Aroife near Arras, in the province of Artois in France.

DURING the fpace of two hundred years after its erection, this abbey was almoft every year acquiring frefh additions of wealth and power, by the donations of diverfe Noblemen, Bifhops and Barons, befides many rich oblations daily made by perfons of every rank. Among

ADDENDA TO VOL. II.

BERWICKSHIRE.

LITTLE DEN TOWER.

LITTLE DEN TOWER was a fortalice or Border-houfe belonging to the Kers; it is pleafantly fituated on a cliff, overlooking the river Tweed. It is now entirely in ruins, and is the property of —— Ker, of Newhorn, Efq.—See the view facing page 114. Vol. I.

ADDENDA TO THRIEVE CASTLE, GALLOWAY.

THE information of Robert Smith, formerly of the parifh of Dunfcore, in the fheriffdom of Dumfries:

THAT as we were paffing by the Old Caftle of Treve (where his late Majefty of bleffed memory had a garrifon in the beginning of the unhappy troubles of his reign) old —— Gordon of Earlftown (who in a few days after was killed at Bothwell Bridge) in my hearing fpoke to the officers that were about him as followeth—" Gentlemen, I was the man that commanded the party which took this caftle from the late king, who had in it about two hundred of the name of Maxwell, of whom the greateft part being papifts, we put them all to the fword, and demolifhed the caftle as you fee it: and now (though an old man) I take up arms againft the fon, whom I hope to fee go the fame way that his father went: for we can never put truft in a covenant breaker: fo, gentlemen, your caufe is good, you need not fear to fight againft a forfworn king."—*Rye-houfe Plot.*

diverse remarkable donations of fisheries, pasturage, &c. was one granted by the founder King David, of half the skins and tallow of all the beasts slain for the king's use at Stirling.

During the wars with England, in the reign of David Bruce, this monastery was pillaged of its most valuable furniture. To replace this loss, William Deladel, Bishop of St. Andrews, made a grant to this community of the vicarage of Clackmannan. In 1559, the monastery was spoiled, and great part of the fabric cast down by the Reformers; several of the monks embraced the reformation, but on that account had their portions prohibited by the Queen Regent.

Mr. David Panther was the last ecclesiastic, who possessed this lucrative abbotship. During the commotions attending the reformation, church benefices were often seized on by those in power, without any lawful authority. John, Earl of Marr, afterwards Regent, (according to Mr. Nimmo) assumed the disposal of the revenues of this abbey, if he did not actually possess a considerable part of them : he had, during the reign of James V. been appointed commendator of Inch Mahome Priory, which, together with that of Rosneth in Dunbartonshire, were dependent on Cambuskenneth. After the reformation had taken place, we find Adam Erskine, one of his nephews, commendator of Cambuskenneth. Moreover the earl himself carried off the stones of the fabric to build his own house, still called Marr's work, in the town of Stirling.

In 1562, by virtue of an order from Queen Mary and the privy council, an account was taken of all the revenues belonging to cathedrals, abbies, priories, and other religious houses, that stipends might be modified to the reformed clergy, who were to have a third of the benefices. According to that account, the revenues of Cambuskenneth were as follows: 930l. 13s. 4½d. Scots money; 11 chalders, 11 bolls, 2 firlots of wheat; 28 chalders, 12 bolls, 3 firlots, 3 pecks, 2 lippies of bear; 31 chalders, 6 bolls, 3 firlots, 3 pecks, 2 lippies of meal; 19 chalders, 15 bolls, 3 firlots, 3 pecks, 2 lippies of oats : in whole, 91 chalders, 15 bolls, 1 firlot, 2 pecks, 2 lippies.

After the accession of James VI. to the crown of England, the temporality of Cambuskenneth, together with that of Dryburgh, and the

priory

priory of Inch Mahome, were conferred to John Earl of Marr, fon of the regent, that, to ufe the terms of the grant, he might be in a better condition to provide for his youngeft fons, whom he had by a lady, Mary Stewart, daughter of the Duke of Lennox, and a relation to his Majefty. The barony of Cambufkenneth, in which the monaftery was fituated, was fettled by the Earl on Alexander Erfkine, one of his fons, who dying without iffue, it came to Charles Erfkine, of Alva, his brother, whofe pofterity continued in the poffeffion of it till about the year 1737, when it was purchafed by the town-council of Stirling, for the benefit of Cowan's hofpital, to which it ftill belongs.

This abbey was once an extenfive building, but nothing of it at prefent remains, except a few broken walls, the bell tower, and ftaircafe, which tower has lately been barbaroufly fmeared over with whiting: fome remains of the garden are alfo to be feen, and the burial place of K. James and his Queen: no traces of the church remain. One of the bells belonging to the monaftery is faid to have been for fome time in Stirling; but, as tradition goes, the fineft was loft in the river, as they were tranfporting it.

Several parliaments were held in this monaftery, and here in 1326 the clergy, earls, and barons, with a great number of an inferior rank, fwore fealty to David Bruce; and at the fame time here was folemnized the marriage between Andrew Murray, of Bothwell, and Chriftan Bruce, fifter to King Robert.

Many of the abbots of this houfe were men of eminence in the political as well as literary line.

FINIS.

T. Brafley, Printer,
Bell Court, Fleet Street, London.

COUNTY INDEX, VOL. II.

ABERDEENSHIRE.

	Page
Aberdeen Cathedral Church	96—98

ANGUSSHIRE.

Aberbroth Abbey and Tower, Plate I.	88—92
———— Plate II.	93
Brechen Cathedral Church	93—95
Glames Caftle, Plate I.	86—88
———— Plate II.	88
Red Caftle	95
Reftennote Priory	95

ARGYLESHIRE.

Dunftaffage Caftle, Lorne	125, 126

AYRSHIRE.

Alloway Church	31—33
Auchinleck Old Caftle or Manfion	43, 44
Colaine or Culzeen Caftle	41, 42
Corfhill Houfe	47
Crofraguel Abbey, Plate I.	34—39
———— Plate II.	39
———— Plate III.	39
Dean Caftle	46, 47
Dolquharran Caftle	30
Dunure Caftle, Plate I.	28, 29
———— Plate II.	29
Greenand Caftle	30
Kilwinning Abbey	44—46
Machlin Caftle	42
Maybole or Minniboil Collegiate Church	25, 26
Old Houfe of Caffils	29
Paifley Abbey, Renfrewfhire	47—50

	Page
St. John the Baptist's Church	26—28
Sorne Castle	43
Turnbury Castle	40, 41

BANFFSHIRE.

Boyne Castle, Plate I.	103
———— Plate II.	103
Inchdrewr Castle	104

BERWICKSHIRE.

Little Den Tower, (*See Addenda*, p. 137, Vol II.)—The View placed facing page 114, Vol. I.

CLACKMANNANSHIRE.

Clackmannan Tower	57

FIFESHIRE.

Balmerino Abbey	116, 117
Black Friars, or the Dominicans, St. Andrew's	122
Castle of St. Andrews	122, 123
Cathedral Church, St Andrews	121, 122
Den Miln Castle	124
Dumfermling Abbey, Plate I.	117—120
———————— Plate II.	120
Dumfermling Fratery	120
Pittenweem Priory	114, 115
Roseythe Castle	115, 116

GALLOWAY.

Abbots Tower, near New Abbey	11
Butel Castle	12
Dundrennan Abbey, Plate I.	12, 13
———————— Plate II.	14
Dunskey Castle, Plate I.	23, 24
———— Plate II.	24
Glenluce Abbey, Plate I.	14, 15
———————— Plate II.	15
	Kenmure

COUNTY INDEX, VOL. II.

	Page
Kenmure Caftle, Plate I.	21, 22
——————— Plate II.	22
Kennedy Caftle, Wigtonfhire	23
Kirkcudbright Caftle, Plate I.	19—21
——————— Plate II.	21
Laggan Stone, Plate I.	22
——————— Plate II.	22, 23
Lincluden College, Plate I.	1—5
——————— Plate II.	5
Loch Roicton, or Hill Caftle	17, 18
Mote of Urr, (Galloway *on the plate*) Plate I.	11, 12
——————— Plate II.	12
New Abbey, or Sweethearts, Plate I.	8—12
——————— Plate II.	12
Thrieve, or Thrieff Caftle (*See Addenda*, p. 137)	5—8

KINCARDINESHIRE.

Dunotter Caftle	99—102

KINROSS-SHIRE.

Loch Leven Caftle	57—60
Lochor Caftle	60, 61

LINLITHGOWSHIRE.

Linlithgow Palace	63—65

MORAYSHIRE.

Bifhop's Palace, at Spynie, Plate I.	112, 113
——————— Plate II.	113
Elgin Cathedral Church, Plate I.	105—109
——————— Plate II.	109
Plufcardin Priory	110—112

PERTHSHIRE.

Abernethy College, Plate I,	83—85
——————— Plate II.	85

Campbell

	Page
Campbell Caftle, Plate I. *(See Addenda,* p. 137, 138)	79, 80
——————— Plate II.	80
Culrofs or Kyllenrofs Abbey	80—82
Doun Caftle	75
Dunblane Cathedral	82, 83
Elcho Caftle	79
Gowrie Houfe or Caftle	76
Hunting Tower	77—79
Monks Tower	76, 77

RENFREWSHIRE.

Newark Caftle	126

STIRLINGSHIRE.

Almond Houfe	66
Bruce's Caftle	66
Emanuel or Manuel Nunnery	67, 68
Cembufkenneth Abbey	138
Stirling Church, or the Grey Friars	72—74
Stirling Caftle	68—72

TWEEDALE.

Auchincafs Caftle, Evandale	55
Crofs Church, Peebles	51—53
Drummelzier Caftle, Tweedale	56
Nid-Path Caftle	54, 55
St. Andrew's Church, Peebles	53, 54
Tweedmuir Church	56

ISLANDS.

Brodie Caftle, Ifle of Arran	127
Ranza Caftle, Ifle of Arran	127
Dunvegan Caftle, Ifle of Sky	128—130
Inch Colm Abbey, Plate I.	131—136
——————— Plate II.	136
——————— Plate III.	136

www.ingramcontent.com/pod-product-compliance
Lightning Source LLC
Chambersburg PA
CBHW020255170426
43202CB00008B/376